The Giant Book of Cool Facts

By
Jake Jacobs

Kindle Edition

* * * * *

Published by Jake Jacobs at Amazon Kindle

The Giant Book of Cool Facts
Copyright© 2018 by Jake Jacobs

1.

During World War II, if a U.S. submarine sank all the targets it engaged, it was considered a "clean sweep" and a broom was attached to the periscope to celebrate their accomplishment.

Reference: (https://en.wikipedia.org/wiki/Clean_sweep_(naval))

2.

Actor Terrance Howard has an insane mathematical theory that 1x1=2, not 1.

Reference: (https://mashable.com/2015/09/14/terrence-howard-one-times-one/#JsRQ9xy4p5qH)

3.

Antoinette Tuff is an office worker who in 2013 talked down a man who had opened fire in her school.

Reference: (https://www.cnn.com/2013/08/21/us/georgia-school-gunshots/index.html)

4.

In Islam, there is a special category of men and women who memorize the whole Qur'an.

Reference: (https://en.wikipedia.org/wiki/Hafiz_%28Quran%29)

5.

The single game scoring record for March Madness is 61 points by Austin Carr, before there was a three point line.

Reference: (https://theundefeated.com/features/austin-carr-ncaa-tournament-scoring-records/)

6.

Robert Smalls was a slave who freed himself, his crew and their families by overtaking Confederate ship, CSS Planter, and sailing it north. The ship contained a code book letting them pass CSA checkpoints. He became the new captain of the ship and convinced Abraham Lincoln to admit African Americans to the Army.

Reference: (https://en.wikipedia.org/wiki/Robert_Smalls#Service_to_the_Union)

7.

Kansas City, Missouri, which was named in 1853, existed before the state of Kansas, which got statehood in 1861, and before Kansas City, Kansas, which was named in 1872, right across the street.

Reference: (https://en.wikipedia.org/wiki/Kansas_City,_Missouri)

8.

With the exception of the United States and Canada, most countries have adopted and use the ISO standard for paper sizes. While Mexico, Panama, Venezuela, Colombia, the Philippines, and Chile have officially adopted the ISO standard, they still use the U.S. standard.

Reference: (https://en.wikipedia.org/wiki/ISO_216#Application)

9.

Saturn has 62 moons and moonlets, 9 of which don't have names.

Reference: (https://en.wikipedia.org/wiki/Moons_of_Saturn)

10.

A 34C bra size is the equivalent of a 36B, 32D, 38A and 30E.

Reference: (https://www.thirdlove.com/blogs/unhooked/sister-sizes-the-bra-secret-every-woman-should-know)

11.

Chester Bennington's final purchase before his death was a new house in Los Angeles with five bedrooms and four bathrooms, priced at $4 million. Many people believe this may have been him trying to make sure his family were secure before his passing.

Reference: (https://www.independent.co.uk/arts-entertainment/music/news/chester-bennington-dead-linkin-park-suicide-set-up-family-a7861261.html)

12.

20 first responders performed CPR on a dying man for more than an hour and a half until paramedics arrived. He survived.

Reference: (https://www.npr.org/2011/08/22/139670971/when-not-to-quit-man-revived-after-96-minutes)

13.

At the start of Operation Good Hope, U.S. forces were supposed to land on the beaches of Mogadishu under the cover of darkness. Instead, they were met by CNN who was covering the landing live on television.

Reference: (https://www.youtube.com/watch?v=Xj9Fn3qG-Cw)

14.

Nazis in World War II used a killing device called the "Genickschussanlage" to fake being a concentration camp doctor pretending to measure the prisoner's height, only to allow another soldier to shoot the standing prisoner in the neck through a hole in the wall.

Reference: (https://en.wikipedia.org/wiki/Buchenwald_concentration_camp#Causes_of_death)

15.

FM radio stations end in odd numbers to reduce interference.

Reference: (https://www.interestinganswers.com/history/fm-radio-stations-end-odd-numbers/)

16.

Charlie Chaplin sued an impersonator, a Mexican actor who went by the stage name "Charlie Aplin."

Reference: (http://mentalfloss.com/article/66364/charlie-chaplin-once-sued-imposter-named-charlie-aplin)

17.

A Soviet Russia Colonel saved the world from World War III by choosing not to fire a nuclear missile at the United States.

Reference: (http://www.abc.net.au/news/2017-09-19/stanislav-petrov,-who-saved-the-world-from-nuclear-war,-dies/8960296)

18.

Making eye contact with an infant makes adults' and babies' brainwaves "get in sync" with each other, which is likely to support communication and learning, according to researchers at the University of Cambridge.

Reference: (https://www.cam.ac.uk/research/news/eye-contact-with-your-baby-helps-synchronise-your-brainwaves)

19.

Great Britain passed the Quebec Act of 1774, respecting Catholicism and French civil law, because they worried French settlers would revolt. The act also gave land west of the Thirteen Colonies to Quebec, angering Colonials and precipitating the American Revolution. The French never revolted.

Reference: (https://en.wikipedia.org/wiki/Quebec_Act)

20.

The tiny African nation of Djibouti has more foreign military bases that any other country in the world.

Reference: (https://www.politico.eu/blogs/the-coming-wars/2018/01/the-most-valuable-military-real-estate-in-the-world/)

21.

Carl Laemmle migrated to the United States in 1884. He started one of the first movie theaters in Chicago, challenged Thomas Edison's monopoly on films, began advertising stars to increase their earnings, founded Universal and sponsored hundreds of Jews to emigrate from Nazi Germany to the U.S.

Reference: (https://en.wikipedia.org/wiki/Carl_Laemmle)

22.

The Hitomi X-ray telescope exploded in space due to a software bug that caused it to compensate for a rotation it didn't have. This overcompensation caused a snowball effect which ultimately caused the satellite to spin out of control and explode.

Reference: (https://en.wikipedia.org/wiki/Hitomi_(satellite))

23.

At one point, 90% of the world's needles came from a Worcestershire town called Redditch.

Reference: (http://www.itv.com/news/central/2014-04-16/50-things-about-new-town-redditch-on-its-50th-birthday/)

24.

North-Korea still has not paid Sweden for the 600 Volvos they bought in 1971.

Reference: (https://en.wikipedia.org/wiki/North_Korea%E2%80%93Sweden_relations)

25.

The commercial brewing of beer has taken place since at least 2500 BC. In ancient Mesopotamia, brewer's derived social sanction and divine protection from the goddess Ninkasi.

Reference: (https://en.wikipedia.org/wiki/Brewery)

26.

Dry cleaning is not a "dry" process: clothes are soaked in a solvent other than water.

Reference: (https://en.wikipedia.org/wiki/Dry_cleaning)

27.

France built a second Paris during World War I to fool the Germans.

Reference: (https://www.telegraph.co.uk/news/worldnews/europe/france/8879053/Second-Paris-built-towards-end-of-First-World-War-to-fool-Germans.html)

28.

The corned beef many people eat on St. Patrick's Day is actually Jewish corned beef, not Irish corned beef.

Reference: (https://www.smithsonianmag.com/arts-culture/is-corned-beef-really-irish-2839144/)

29.

A snail known as the geography cone is the most venomous animal on Earth. Its venom is a mix of hundreds of toxins delivered through a harpoon-like tooth, and there's no anti-venom.

Reference: (https://en.wikipedia.org/wiki/Conus_geographus)

30.

7 feet tall people are so rare that if you know an American man between 20 and 40 who is 7 feet tall, there's a 17% chance he's in the NBA.

Reference: (https://www.youtube.com/watch?v=8COaMKbNrX0)

31.

Unschooling believes in students learning through their natural life experiences including play, household responsibilities, personal interests and curiosity, internships and work experience, travel, books, elective classes, family, mentors, and social interaction.

Reference: (https://en.wikipedia.org/wiki/Unschooling)

32.

Guinness World Records lists Agatha Christie as the best-selling novelist of all time. Selling 2 billion copies, her estate claims that her works come third in the rankings of the world's most-widely published books, behind only Shakespeare's works and the Bible.

Reference: (https://en.wikipedia.org/wiki/Agatha_Christie)

33.

French chemist Louis Jacques Thénard discovered hydrogen peroxide in 1818.

Reference: (https://en.wikipedia.org/wiki/Louis_Jacques_Th%C3%A9nard)

34.

Socrates was very worried that the increasing use of books in education would have the effect of ruining students' ability to memorize things. We only remember this now because Plato wrote it down.

Reference: (http://www.liberalarts.wabash.edu/lao-1-3-socrates-on-technology)

35.

One of the forebears of Jeremy Clarkson were the inventors of the Kilner Jars.

Reference: (http://www.bbc.co.uk/whodoyouthinkyouare/past-stories/jeremy-clarkson.shtml)

36.

An identity thief stole the identity of a surgeon and while aboard a Navy destroyer was tasked with performing several lifesaving surgeries. He proceeded to memorize a medical textbook just before hand and successfully performed the surgery with all patients surviving.

Reference: (https://en.wikipedia.org/wiki/Ferdinand_Waldo_Demara#Impersonations)

37.

Naqsha Bibi survived 63 days trapped in a kneeling position in her kitchen after the 2005 Kashmir Earthquake.

Reference: (https://www.telegraph.co.uk/news/worldnews/asia/pakistan/1505472/Woman-found-alive-63-days-after-earthquake.html)

38.

The richest person in Hong Kong is a high school dropout who first started a plastic flower company in 1950.

Reference: (https://en.wikipedia.org/wiki/Li_Ka-shing)

39.

Rudy Kurniawan sold regular wine in fancy bottles and made millions of dollars, only to get thrown in jail for "Wine Fraud".

Reference: (https://en.wikipedia.org/wiki/Rudy_Kurniawan)

40.

People diagnosed with Alzheimer's disease may lose the ability to smell peanut butter. The "Peanut Butter Test" may offer an early indication of the disease.

Reference: (https://health.clevelandclinic.org/peanut-butter-test-may-detect-alzheimers/)

41.

The total biomass of all the ants in the world is approximately equal to the total biomass of the entire human race.

Reference: (https://wikipedia.org/wiki/Ant#Relationship_with_humans)

42.

LEGO model makers rely on solvents to weld blocks together rather than using glue.

Reference: (http://thebrickblogger.com/2011/01/lego-glued-magnet-removal/)

43.

29,000 rubber ducks helped model the ocean current.

Reference: (https://en.wikipedia.org/wiki/Friendly_Floatees)

44.

Kodak invented the digital camera in 1975, but the executives suppressed it so as not to hurt their camera film revenue.

Reference: (http://uk.businessinsider.com/this-man-invented-the-digital-camera-in-1975-and-his-bosses-at-kodak-never-let-it-see-the-light-of-day-2015-8)

45.

The saying "there's safety in numbers" does not describe the likelihood of us surviving when we're in danger. Rather, it describes the change in our perception of that potential threat.

Reference: (https://msutoday.msu.edu/news/2013/whether-human-or-hyena-theres-safety-in-numbers/)

46.

Japanese anime characters are purposely made to look racially ambiguous, in a concept called "mukokuseki".

Reference: (http://allthetropes.wikia.com/wiki/Mukokuseki)

47.

Daft Punk's Grammy award-winning album "Random Access Memories" had its album launch in the tiny Australian town of Wee Waa, with a population of less than 1,700. All 4,000 tickets were sold out within 13 minutes.

Reference: (http://www.news.com.au/entertainment/music/daft-punk-to-launch-new-record-in-wee-waa/news-story/b3b7cdeffa5ce9984d5e3d58858872ad)

48.

Using an ejection seat carries a high risk of spinal injury. They are used only when absolutely necessary to avoid imminent death.

Reference: (https://www.researchgate.net/figure/Probability-of-spinal-injury-estimated-from-operational-ejection-seat-experience-35_fig2_260310327)

49.

Salem Poor was a slave who purchased his freedom, and fought in the battle of Bunker Hill. His actions earned him the praise of 14 officers who called him, "a brave and gallant soldier".

Reference: (https://en.wikipedia.org/wiki/Salem_Poor)

50.

In 1885, kids attending the White House Easter Egg Roll snuck into the East Room, hoping to meet President Cleveland. They trashed the place, ruining the East Room carpet, which was ground full of freshly smashed hard-boiled egg and broken egg shells.

Reference: (http://www.cnhinews.com/cnhi/article_7a7a4c72-237c-11e7-9fc3-8719472cbd47.html)

51.

Many Detroit residents believe in a trickster; a red imp that causes a constant cycle of prosperity and disaster for the city. This belief goes back to French settlers and even the native tribes. They even hold an annual costume parade as both a tribute and a warning.

Reference: (http://michigansotherside.com/the-red-dwarf-of-detroit-or-the-nain-rouge/)

52.

Baby koala's find eucalyptus leaves too toxic while they're growing so they feast on their mother's feces until they can handle the leaves.

Reference: (https://pickle.nine.com.au/2015/07/24/13/17/koala-pap)

53.

Michael Cera played the voice of "Little Gizmo" from the 2003 children's show "Rolie Polie Olie".

Reference: (https://en.wikipedia.org/wiki/Rolie_Polie_Olie#Voice_cast)

54.

In the years following the John F. Kennedy assassination, when she found herself in need of money, Lee Harvey Oswald's mother would go to Dealey Plaza and sell her autograph to tourists.

Reference: (https://www.smithsonianmag.com/history/when-lee-harvey-oswald-shot-president-his-mother-tried-take-center-stage-180953351/)

55.

Steve Urkel's catchphrase, "Did I do that?", was taken from the 1934 Three Stooges short, "Punch Drunks".

Reference: (https://en.wikipedia.org/wiki/Punch_Drunks)

56.

Horses walk around on their middle fingers.

Reference: (https://thehorse.com/149565/where-did-horses-extra-toes-go/)

57.

Since The Croatian War of Independence ended in 1995, over 500 civilians have died, and nearly 1,500 have been injured within the 157 square miles of minefields that are still active in Croatia.

Reference: (https://en.wikipedia.org/wiki/Minefields_in_Croatia)

58.

In 1859, an American farmer in the San Juan Islands shot a pig who was eating his potatoes, but the pig happened to belong to a British colonist. The conflict escalated to involve 461 Americans and 14 artillery against 5 British warships with 70 cannons and 2,140 men. The only casualty was the pig.

Reference: (https://en.wikipedia.org/wiki/Pig_War_(1859))

59.

The Greek philosopher Chrysippus allegedly died by laughing at his own joke.

Reference: (https://en.wikipedia.org/wiki/Chrysippus)

60.

The name LEGO comes from the Danish "leg godt" which means "play well".

Reference: (https://en.wikipedia.org/wiki/Lego#History)

61.

The Bristol Stool Scale is a medical classification of human feces that includes categories such as "like a smooth, soft sausage," "soft blobs with clear cut edges," and "mushy consistency with ragged edges."

Reference: (https://en.wikipedia.org/wiki/Bristol_stool_scale)

62.

The first animals in space were fruit flies.

Reference: (https://amp.space.com/20648-animals-in-space-history-infographic.html)

63.

In 2014, highly trained snipers nearly knocked out power to Silicon Valley and were never caught.

Reference: (https://www.npr.org/sections/thetwo-way/2014/02/05/272015606/sniper-attack-on-calif-power-station-raises-terrorism-fears)

64.

In 1909. at a world's fair in Seattle, a month-old orphaned boy named Ernest was raffled away as a prize. A winning ticket was drawn but nobody claimed the prize. Ernest's destiny is still being investigated.

Reference:(https://en.wikipedia.org/wiki/Alaska%E2%80%93Yukon%E2%80%93Pacific_Exposition)

65.

The famous headline "Foot Heads Arms Body", published after Michael Foot was chosen to be the chair of a nuclear disarmament committee, was written by a sub editor as a joke and was never intended to be published.

Reference: (https://www.theguardian.com/theguardian/2010/mar/05/footnotes-life-michael-foot)

66.

Jim Parsons thought "The Big Bang Theory" was a game show before auditioning for it. He confused Chuck Lorre with Chuck Woolery, who was the original host of "Wheel of Fortune."

Reference: (http://mentalfloss.com/article/68129/13-smart-facts-about-big-bang-theory)

67.

The ITV color strike is an industrial action in the early 1970s that lead to several shows having to be broadcast in black and white.

Reference: (https://en.wikipedia.org/wiki/Colour_Strike)

68.

Bryan Cranston and his brother were suspected of murdering their boss and wanted by the police in the 1970s. They had previously joked about killing him and his actual murder coincided with the Cranston brothers leaving town on their motorcycles. They were cleared days later.

Reference: (https://www.gq.com/story/bryan-cranston-murder-suspect)

69.

Because Hawaii is rabies-free, they have a quarantine law on cats and dogs who do not comply with Hawaii's import requirements.

Reference: (http://hdoa.hawaii.gov/ai/aqs/animal-quarantine-information-page/)

70.

China consumes 25 million trees worth of chopsticks every year.

Reference: (https://en.wikipedia.org/wiki/Chopsticks)

71.

The flag on the Moon has a horizontal pole at the top to support it and make it look like it is flying.

Reference: (https://en.wikipedia.org/wiki/Lunar_Flag_Assembly)

72.

334 people died during a 3-day-long school siege in Belsan, Russia. 186 of those deaths were children.

Reference: (https://en.wikipedia.org/wiki/Beslan_school_siege)

73.

Madeleine Astor, a woman who lost her husband in the Titanic disaster, inherited $114 million, was denied her heritage because she got married again, divorced from her second marriage to marry an abusive Italian, only to be sent to jail for bigamy and die from an overdose at 47 years old.

Reference: (https://www.independent.co.uk/arts-entertainment/books/features/curse-of-the-titanic-what-happened-to-those-who-survived-6252311.html)

74.

Michael Jackson worked with Stephen King to create a short film called "Ghosts." It set the world record for the longest music video at 40 minutes and centered on Michael Jackson as a rich recluse in a town where the adults try to run him out and he ends up being saved by children.

Reference: (http://stephenking.wikia.com/wiki/Michael_Jackson%27s_Ghosts)

75.

Architects tried to raise $2.9 billion to build Minas Tirith, the city in "Lord of the Rings".

Reference: (http://bgr.com/2015/08/13/lord-of-the-rings-minas-tirith-indiegogo/)

76.

A dog in Mexico named Frida has identified and saved the lives of 12 people trapped under rubble from earthquakes, and has identified a total of 52 bodies during her career. She is now considered a national heroine in Mexico.

Reference: (http://time.com/4954826/frida-rescue-dog-mexico-city-earthquake/)

77.

LeBron James has a photographic memory and is able to remember exact in-game scenarios in basketball games he has played throughout his career over the years; growing up he was able to memorize moves in fighting games so well that his friends thought he was cheating.

Reference: (http://www.espn.com/nba/story/_/id/11067098/lebron-james-greatest-weapon-brain)

78.

The Heaven's Gate cult, who committed mass suicide in 1997, had rules against even thinking about sex. It got so bad that some male members opted to get castrated. One male member, said he flipped a coin with another member and the "winner" would get to be castrated.

Reference: (https://www.youtube.com/watch?v=9qgjObjUQkg&t=217s)

79.

The first registered internet domain name was Symbolics.com, it was registered May 15th, 1985.

Reference: (https://en.wikipedia.org/wiki/Symbolics)

80.

Former Rutgers Men's Basketball coach Mike Rice Jr., was caught on video tape physically abusing his players at practice.

Reference: (https://en.wikipedia.org/wiki/Mike_Rice_Jr.)

81.

Some common Swifts, a type of bird, can fly for 10 months without landing.

Reference: (https://www.nature.com/news/record-breaking-common-swifts-fly-for-10-months-without-landing-1.20873)

82.

Lack of sleep may cause Alzheimer's.

Reference: (https://www.alzheimers.net/2013-10-29/lack-of-sleep-may-cause-alzheimers/)

83.

3 years ago, Miami Dade College reached a $33.5 million settlement with the contractor and subcontractors hired to build a parking garage at the Doral campus that collapsed during construction killing four people and injuring seven others.

Reference: (http://www.miamiherald.com/news/local/community/miami-dade/doral/article20700564.html)

84.

Matashichi Oishi, a crew member involved in the Lucky Dragon No. 5 incident, reported that he "took a lick" of the nuclear fallout dust that fell on the ship and described it as, "gritty but with no taste".

Reference: (https://en.wikipedia.org/wiki/Daigo_Fukury%C5%AB_Maru)

85.

Giant pandas were removed from the Endangered Species list.

Reference: (https://en.wikipedia.org/wiki/Giant_panda)

86.

It's disrespectful not to burn an American flag once it's worn out.

Reference: (https://en.wikipedia.org/wiki/United_States_Flag_Code)

87.

Switzerland banned the practice of boiling lobsters alive because scientific research proved that they can feel pain, and that chefs justify this practice by the fact that lobsters' meat goes bad very fast so they have to be boiled alive to keep it tasty.

Reference: (http://ponderwall.com/index.php/2018/01/12/switzerland-bans-boiling-lobsters-alive/)

88.

The Doris Miller Department of Veterans Affairs Medical Center in Waco, Texas, was originally a veteran's mental facility and is named after Doris Miller, a Waco native, who manned a gun and shot down 4 enemy aircraft during the raid on Pearl Harbor.

Reference: (https://www.centraltexas.va.gov/about/Waco.asp)

89.

There is an "inner" part of garlic that can be removed to avoid it becoming bitter.

Reference: (https://www.thekitchn.com/bitter-garlic-just-remove-the-141639)

90.

Graham Russell of the band Air Supply was a left handed guitarist who played his instrument upside down. Most left handed musicians would re-string right handed guitars backwards to compensate, but he plays with the low E string on the bottom.

Reference: (https://www.youtube.com/watch?v=JWdZEumNRmI&feature=youtu.be)

91.

Roland had to stop producing the TR-808 because it could no longer buy defective transistors.

Reference: (https://www.newyorker.com/culture/culture-desk/the-808-heard-round-the-world)

92.

27% of Canadian males considers themselves feminist.

Reference: (http://www.macleans.ca/the-canada-project-24-facts/#feminism)

93.

In "The Wizard of Oz," Scarecrow had a gun.

Reference: (https://www.youtube.com/watch?v=p9hcXm2vr5I&feature=youtu.be)

94.

The large animal detection system onboard Volvo's driverless car didn't know how big or how far away the Kangaroos were, when the car was tested in Australia.

Reference: (http://www.abc.net.au/news/2017-06-24/driverless-cars-in-australia-face-challenge-of-roo-problem/8574816)

95.

20th Century Fox, in the 1950s, had plans to develop 260 acres of their property into commercial real estate. However, its studio head scrapped that idea and decided to sell the land for $43 million to finance the movie "Cleopatra". That land became Century City and is now worth $6.4 billion.

Reference: (https://www.hollywoodreporter.com/features/why-century-city-ranks-worst-635438)

96.

North Korea attacked and hijacked a U.S. Navy spy ship. They keep it as a war museum.

Reference: (https://www.history.com/this-day-in-history/uss-pueblo-captured)

97.

There was a short-lived 1977 buddy cop TV series about a small town Irish cop who fights crime with the help of his best friend the local rabbi using his "rabbinic mind" and Talmudic training.

Reference: (https://en.wikipedia.org/wiki/Lanigan%27s_Rabbi)

98.

If a guide dog owner needs assistance they will let their harness handle lie flat on their guide dog's back.

Reference: (https://www.guidedogs.org.uk/guide-dogs-in-school/puppy-resources/guide-dogs-in-the-community/sighted-guiding/)

99.

TUI, the German travel company, formerly called Preussag AG, used to sell chemical weapons to Iraq before the Gulf War.

Reference: (http://www.nytimes.com/2002/12/21/world/threats-responses-suppliers-declaration-lists-companies-that-sold-chemicals-iraq.html)

100.

From 1943 to 1947, part of the Manhattan Project involved injecting radioactive polonium into terminally ill patients at hospitals to study its fatal effects.

Reference: (https://en.wikipedia.org/wiki/Polonium?r=1#Well-known_poisoning_cases)

101.

Translated into Mandarin Chinese, Subway means "taste better than others."

Reference: (https://www.huffingtonpost.com/2014/11/05/facts-about-subway-_n_6095206.html)

102.

There's a colony of wallabies on the Hawaiian island of Oahu. The colony started when 2 escaped from a private zoo in 1916. You probably won't see any because they're incredibly rare, although they have been captured on video.

Reference: (http://www.khon2.com/news/local-news/caught-on-video-the-elusive-kalihi-valley-wallaby/1025937619)

103.

The FIAT Lingotto factory had a test track on its roof.

Reference: (https://jalopnik.com/5714628/fiats-roof-top-test-track)

104.

Migos, the rap group, are all related. Quavo is Takeoff's uncle, and Offset is Quavo's cousin.

Reference:(https://en.wikipedia.org/w/index.php?title=Migos&mobileaction=toggle_view_desktop#History)

105.

Finis Bates wrote a book about John Wilkes Booth and how he may have escaped being killed by Union soldiers.

Reference: (https://en.wikipedia.org/wiki/Finis_L._Bates)

106.

The blue whale has an average penis size of 8 to 10 feet and produces about 10 gallons of sperm while ejaculating.

Reference: (http://www.whalefacts.org/blue-whale-penis/)

107.

There's a blood donor scheme for dogs in the U.K.

Reference: (https://www.petbloodbankuk.org/)

108.

In 1976, Jodie Foster starred in 5 feature films, winning 2 Baftas, an Oscar nomination, and countless other awards. She was 13 years old.

Reference: (https://en.wikipedia.org/wiki/Jodie_Foster)

109.

During the Year of the Dragon there is a baby boom due to "dragon babies" being considered auspicious.

Reference: (https://www.aeaweb.org/conference/2018/preliminary/paper/RG5a4EbD)

110.

All of the music on Mr. Rogers was performed live off screen.

Reference: (https://en.wikipedia.org/wiki/Johnny_Costa)

111.

When the first telephone was installed in the White House during the presidency of Rutherford B. Hayes, it was only connected to the Treasury Department and was assigned the telephone number "1".

Reference: (https://www.history.com/this-day-in-history/hayes-has-first-phone-installed-in-white-house)

112.

Kit Kat was originally the name of a seventeenth century literary and political club that met in the pie shop of a pastry cook called Christopher Catling; Mr. Catling's names being more easily shortened to Kit and Cat.

Reference: (https://www.nestle.co.uk/aboutus/history/kitkat-is-named-after-a-man-called-christopher)

113.

Long before their major success, Marvel Studios risked almost all of their remaining major properties such as The Avengers for a $525 million financing deal with Merrill Lynch.

Reference: (http://screencrush.com/marvel-bankruptcy-billions/)

114.

Earth is located in the Orion Arm of the Milky Way in the Laniakea Supercluster.

Reference:(http://www.slate.com/blogs/bad_astronomy/2014/09/04/laniakea_our_local_supercluster.html)

115.

In 1983, a man willfully spilt red paint over the Canadian Constitution Act to, "graphically illustrate to Canadians", how wrong the government was to allow U.S. cruise missile testing in Canada. He was later sentenced to just 89 days in weekend jail.

Reference: (http://www.cbc.ca/archives/entry/1984-missile-protester-sentenced-for-defacing-constitution)

116.

To launch the first exhibit of life-sized dinosaur models, a banquet was held in the Iguanodon.

Reference: (https://en.wikipedia.org/wiki/Crystal_Palace_Dinosaurs)

117.

At the Tibetan Freedom Concert in 1998, lightning struck the crowd injuring twelve people; four critically.

Reference: (https://en.wikipedia.org/wiki/Tibetan_Freedom_Concert#Washington_D.C._lightning_strike)

118.

There's a state park in Utah named after the type of film used by National Geographic in 1948 to photograph it: "Kodachrome Basin State Park".

Reference: (https://stateparks.utah.gov/parks/kodachrome-basin/)

119.

"The Pirates of Penzance" began with a nursemaid mishearing an order to apprentice a boy as a "pirate" instead of a "pilot". This inspired the Muppet's parody with Gilda Radner asking for a 7-foot talking parrot, and Kermit misinterpreted it as "carrot".

Reference: (https://en.wikipedia.org/wiki/The_Pirates_of_Penzance)

120.

A real life "Red Sparrow": Lilly Barbara Carola Stein was a Nazi spy who was tasked with seducing men in nightclubs, to find intelligence, and then blackmail them.

Reference: (https://en.wikipedia.org/wiki/Duquesne_Spy_Ring)

121.

The bikini was named after a Pacific island the United States bombed during nuclear testing, displacing the entire population and rendering the island uninhabitable. The bikini was supposed to have the same "explosive" effect on men who saw women wearing it.

Reference: (https://en.wikipedia.org/wiki/Bikini)

122.

Women in Ontario are allowed to be topless in public, especially on the streets of Toronto.

Reference: (https://en.wikipedia.org/wiki/Topfreedom_in_Canada)

123.

New knitting patterns were banned in both world wars as a counter-measure to knitted coded messages.

Reference: (https://www.atlasobscura.com/articles/knitting-spies-wwi-wwii)

124.

One of the symptoms of rabies is the fear of water.

Reference: (https://www.healthline.com/health/rabies)

125.

Before the band the "Butthole Surfers" settled on that band name, they went by several other equally strange names, including, "Fred Astaire's Asshole," "The Right To Eat Fred Astaire's Asshole," and "The Inalienable Right To Eat Fred Astaire's Asshole."

Reference: (https://en.wikipedia.org/wiki/Butthole_Surfers)

126.

Buzz Lightyear's original name was Lunar Larry, before being changed to honor astronaut Edwin "Buzz" Aldrin.

Reference: (https://www.independent.co.uk/arts-entertainment/films/news/early-toy-story-concept-art-had-woody-and-buzz-lightyear-looking-a-little-strange-a6792291.html)

127.

The U.S. Military developed a non-lethal "Pain Ray".

Reference: (https://en.wikipedia.org/wiki/Active_Denial_System)

128.

The Dolly Zoom is an in-camera effect achieved by zooming a zoom lens to adjust the angle of view while the camera moves toward or away from the subject in such a way as to keep the subject the same size in the frame throughout. This method is used in many films, most famously in the movie JAWS.

Reference: (https://en.wikipedia.org/wiki/Dolly_zoom)

129.

The Clampett family home was in the Ozarks not Kentucky or Tennessee.

Reference: (https://en.wikipedia.org/wiki/Branson,_Missouri)

130.

In ancient Egypt, baboons were worshiped as gods. They were often portrayed with erections and were prayed in order to ensure that an individual would not suffer from erectile dysfunction after death.

Reference: (https://en.wikipedia.org/wiki/Babi_(mythology))

131.

Mitragynine is an active alkaloid found in the plant Mitragyna speciosa. Recreational users have reported various effects, mainly improved mood and analgesia. Its use is currently unregulated worldwide although the use of the plant in which it is found, is.

Reference: (https://en.wikipedia.org/wiki/Mitragynine)

132.

Michael Swango is a "doctor" that is believed to have poisoned about 60 people on two continents over a span of sixteen years.

Reference: (https://en.wikipedia.org/wiki/Michael_Swango)

133.

There is an island off of Scotland where wallabies have happily inhabited and adapted to the climate there since the 1940s.

Reference: (https://www.scotsman.com/news/the-loch-lomond-island-home-to-wallabies-and-how-to-get-there-1-4205617)

134.

Buddhist cosmology includes a figure like the Christian God. He happened to be born into the world first, and mistakenly believes that he's the all-powerful creator.

Reference: (https://en.wikipedia.org/wiki/Buddhist_cosmology#Brahm%C4%81_worlds)

135.

The term Peanut Gallery came from Vaudeville days when the audience in cheapest and rowdiest seats in the theater often ate peanuts and sometimes threw them at the performers.

Reference: (https://en.wikipedia.org/wiki/Peanut_gallery)

136.

Utah used to have a law which said that drinks must be prepared behind a curtain called a "Zion Curtain" in order to prevent excessive drinking.

Reference: (https://en.wikipedia.org/wiki/Alcohol_laws_of_Utah#Zion_curtains)

137.

"Seinfeld" composer Jonathan Wolff rewrote the theme song for every single episode. He says, "The bassline is so simple it can start and stop for his jokes, hold for laughs, and that way I could architect each piece of music for each monologue, Lego-style."

Reference: (http://www.news.com.au/entertainment/tv/flashback/seinfeld-turns-28-things-you-never-knew-about-the-hit-show/news-story/c96d047b1dea394ef5e86b71b2fe4529)

138.

In Japan, the average homes last for only 30 years due to earthquakes, fires, and World War II.

Reference: (https://www.theguardian.com/sustainable-business/disposable-homes-japan-environment-lifespan-sustainability)

139.

Cinderella is not the real name of the protagonist from the famous story, instead it was an insulting nickname given to her. She was forced to sleep in the ashes and because of that she was always covered in dust and dirt.

Reference: (https://www.pitt.edu/~dash/grimm021.html)

140.

The first back-up camera on a car was in 1956.

Reference: (https://www.cnet.com/pictures/photos-when-gms-designs-ruled-the-road/11/)

141.

Modern hard disk drives have read and write heads that float 4 to 5 nanometers above the surface of the disk while it spins. For scale, a human hair is 80,000 to 100,000 nanometers thick.

Reference: (https://www.nano.gov/nanotech-101/what/nano-size)

142.

The U.S. has technically been a metric nation since 1975 but just hasn't enforced the system onto private companies and people.

Reference: (https://www.law.cornell.edu/uscode/text/15/205b)

143.

During his acceptance speech for the Nobel Prize in 1995, Sir Joseph Rotblat proposed a Hippocratic Oath for Scientists.

Reference: (https://en.wikipedia.org/wiki/Hippocratic_Oath_for_scientists#Joseph_Rotblat)

144.

Competitive nailing is a Bavarian wedding custom for children.

Reference: (https://en.wikipedia.org/wiki/Nagelbalken)

145.

The Wong Fei Hung film series has the most entries in its filmography of a film series; it has 89 films to date.

Reference:(https://en.wikipedia.org/wiki/List_of_feature_film_series_with_more_than_twenty_entries#89)

146.

After being thrown from his horse, jockey Ralph Neves was pronounced dead, brought to the morgue, injected with adrenaline to the heart, jumped up, returned to the racetrack, and demanded to be allowed to ride the rest of his mounts that day.

Reference: (https://en.wikipedia.org/wiki/Ralph_Neves#Death_and_Resurrection)

147.

You can get high on nutmeg. The household spice contains the psychoactive compound myristicin, which can cause hallucinations, euphoria, anxiety, and dizziness.

Reference: (https://www.theatlantic.com/magazine/archive/2012/01/my-nutmeg-bender/308863/)

148.

Ishmael Beah was forced into being a child soldier at the age of 12 in Sierra Leone and he was later rescued at the age of 17. He rehabilitated himself in the U.S, obtained a degree in Political Science, and is now a bestselling author.

Reference: (https://en.wikipedia.org/wiki/Ishmael_Beah)

149.

Luigi Rizzo is nicknamed the Sinker. With his torpedo boat he sank two Austro-Hungarian battleships: SMS Szent István and SMS Wien.

Reference: (https://en.wikipedia.org/wiki/Luigi_Rizzo)

150.

90% of adults have highly contagious Mono lurking in their cells due to a previous infection and it can be transmitted through sharing drinks as well as sexually.

Reference: (https://www.drgreene.com/articles/mononucleosis/)

151.

A jogger in Maine once drowned a rabid raccoon in a puddle after it latched onto her finger and would not release.

Reference: (http://bangordailynews.com/2017/06/14/news/midcoast/maine-woman-attacked-by-raccoon-drowns-rabid-animal-in-puddle/)

152.

While the first savings banks date back ancient Greece, the first piggy banks were made in the 14th century AD in Indonesia.

Reference: (http://www.thehistoryblog.com/archives/20945)

153.

Antony Flew was an English philosopher and a strong advocate of atheism, until, in 2004, he stated to have acknowledged the existence of an Intelligent Creator of the universe, shocking his fellow colleagues and atheists. He was also known for the development of the No True Scotsman Fallacy.

Reference: (https://en.wikipedia.org/wiki/Antony_Flew)

154.

"Ice" beers are standard lagers that are lowered below freezing, and then some of the frozen water is removed to concentrate the beer and increase ABV.

Reference: (http://www.millercoorsblog.com/brewing/ice-beer/)

155.

James Cameron was diving Titanic's wreck as the 9/11 attacks took place, he found out after returning to the surface.

Reference: (http://www.spiegel.de/international/zeitgeist/titanic-director-james-cameron-speaks-about-lasting-fascination-of-ship-a-826121.html)

156.

Winston Churchill was known for his love for sweets, so Hitler had planned to create a chocolate with a bomb inside that would explode upon cracking open a row of chocolate bits.

Reference: (http://www.nationalgeographic.com.au/history/the-nazis-chocolate-bomb-plans.aspx)

157.

Hamlet was translated into Klingon in the mid-1990s.

Reference: (https://shakespeareandbeyond.folger.edu/2016/09/16/shakespeare-klingon-star-trek/)

158.

In a study of 640 dream journals conducted by Harvard University, psychologists determined that the dreams of prisoners in World War II prisoner of war camps were less aggressive than the standard male population. Rather than visions of extreme violence, the majority of soldiers dreamed of escape, family, loneliness, and home.

Reference: (https://news.harvard.edu/gazette/story/2013/10/dream-saga-of-wwii/)

159.

Remarkably, frogs actually use their eyes to help them swallow food. When the frog blinks, its eyeballs are pushed downwards creating a bulge in the roof of its mouth. This bulge squeezes the food inside the frog's mouth down the back of its throat.

Reference: (http://www.sciencekids.co.nz/sciencefacts/animals/frog.html)

160.

The 10-minute behind the scenes stories at the end of the BBC Blue Planet and Planet Earth films were the result of filling in a scheduling shortfall.

Reference: (http://www.independent.co.uk/travel/news-and-advice/adventure-film-academy-teaching-travellers-how-to-make-short-films-anywhere-5328735.html)

161.

Peter J. Ganci, Jr. was the FDNY Chief who died in the 9/11 fires. When it became apparent the building would collapse, he evacuated the others outside the building except for himself and an FDNY Commissioner. Peter refused to leave, saying, "I'm not leaving my men," many of which were still inside.

Reference: (https://en.wikipedia.org/wiki/Peter_J._Ganci_Jr.)

162.

Dogs are actually the same species as wolves and almost all wolves, especially those in Europe, Asia and America, are within the same species with all denominations just being subspecies.

Reference: (https://en.wikipedia.org/wiki/Subspecies_of_Canis_lupus#Disputed_subspecies_and_species)

163.

John I of France is the only French monarch to ever hold the title all his life but also the shortest lived, reigning for only five days.

Reference: (https://en.wikipedia.org/wiki/John_I_of_France)

164.

Abraham Lincoln messed up the first mass-distribution copy of the Gettysburg address, writing on both sides of the paper and making lithograph reproduction impossible. He had to write it out again on two sheets.

Reference: (http://www.abrahamlincolnonline.org/lincoln/speeches/gettysburg.htm)

165.

Ludwig Beck was a German Chief of the General Staff that outwardly criticized Hitler's ambitions and the Munich Agreement before World War II. He had, with other top generals, originally planned to arrest Hitler if he declared war on Czechoslovakia.

Reference: (https://en.wikipedia.org/wiki/Ludwig_Beck)

166.

Operation Flagship was a sting operation that sent out free Redskins tickets to wanted fugitives and resulted in more than 100 arrests with Marshalls wearing Redskins and Chicken costumes.

Reference: (https://www.youtube.com/watch?v=1LsNBA2XwXU&feature=youtu.be)

167.

Human eyes can only show us 2D images. The depth that we all think we can see is merely a trick that our brains have learned.

Reference: (http://sccinfo.usc.edu/geowall/stereohow.html)

168.

Hummingbirds use spiders' webs to glue their nests together.

Reference: (http://www.hummingbirdsociety.org/index-inside.php?Hummingbirds-101-Predators-14)

169.

Charlemagne's grandfather may have stopped a complete Muslim takeover of Europe in 732 A.D.

Reference: (https://en.wikipedia.org/wiki/Charles_Martel)

170.

Ed Helms pulling his own tooth in "The Hangover" was possible because he has one missing tooth that never grew in when he was young so he uses a fake tooth.

Reference: (https://www.youtube.com/watch?v=fpkijZZSrIk&feature=youtu.be&t=140)

171.

The Great Attractor is a gravitational anomaly that is only known due to the fact that it moves galaxies over hundreds of millions of light-years away.

Reference: (https://en.wikipedia.org/wiki/Great_Attractor)

172.

The tongue twister, "she sells seashells by the seashore", is about a real girl named Mary Anning. She also happened to be one of the very first people to discover a massive dinosaur fossil, which she did at the age of 12 while looking for seashells to sell by the seashore.

Reference: (https://lite.my/trending/trending/mary-anning-true-story-tongue-twister-she-sells-se)

173.

The biggest tank battle in history is the little known battle of Brody in 1941.

Reference: (https://en.wikipedia.org/wiki/Battle_of_Brody_(1941))

174.

Flashes of light in the sky often appear before a major earthquake, and can serve as a warning of impending disaster.

Reference: (https://news.nationalgeographic.com/news/2014/01/140106-earthquake-lights-earthquake-prediction-geology-science/)

175.

Chesty Puller once saved a group of Marines trapped behind enemy lines by flagging down a nearby Navy destroyer and directing the actions that would save nearly all of their lives.

Reference: (http://plutarchproject.com/index.php/chesty-puller-a-god-among-mere-mortals/)

176.

After cutting off his ear, Vincent van Gogh painted a portrait of the doctor who treated him, then gave it to the doctor. The doctor hated it and used it to repair a chicken coop before giving it away. It's now worth $50 million.

Reference:(https://en.wikipedia.org/wiki/Vincent_van_Gogh#Hospital_in_Arles_(December_1888))

177.

The country of Liechtenstein has the worst gender ratio in its population. While countries like China are usually thought of having a higher ratio of men to women, Liechtenstein's population imbalance is even greater than China's.

Reference: (https://www.smithsonianmag.com/smart-news/liechtenstein-has-the-most-skewed-ratio-of-baby-boys-and-girls-in-the-world-right-now-8176140/)

178.

The very first trench coat ever invented was by Burberry and was made strictly for crawling and walking through trenches in World War I.

Reference: (http://www.bbc.com/news/uk-england-29033055)

179.

SANDOZ used to sell LSD as a psychiatric drug from the 1940s to the 1960s.

Reference: (https://en.wikipedia.org/wiki/Lysergic_acid_diethylamide#History)

180.

Osama bin Laden left a will that he had written shortly after 9/11 in which he urged his children not to join al-Qaeda and not to continue the Jihad.

Reference: (https://www.theguardian.com/world/2011/may/03/bin-laden-will-wives-children)

181.

People in rural India believe that being bitten by a dog can cause them to become pregnant with puppies. This is called Puppy Pregnancy Syndrome.

Reference: (https://blogs.scientificamerican.com/bering-in-mind/puppy-pregnancy-syndrome-men-who-are-pregnant-with-dogs/)

182.

Weird Al Jankovic suffered from extreme myopia and underwent an image change after getting LASIK, resulting in the glasses-free, moustache less, long-haired appearance for which he is now known.

Reference: (https://en.wikipedia.org/wiki/%22Weird_Al%22_Yankovic)

183.

The song "Be Prepared" from the movie "The Lion King" is sung by two different people. Voice actor Jim Cummings took over after the original Scar actor Jeremy Irons blew his voice out halfway through the song.

Reference: (https://en.wikipedia.org/wiki/Be_Prepared_(Disney_song))

184.

An MLB player sneaked Mission Impossible-style into an umpire's office to replace his teammate's confiscated corked bat with an uncorked one. The heist was quickly discovered as there were, "clumps of ceiling tile on the floor", and the replacement bat had another player's name stenciled on it.

Reference: (https://en.wikipedia.org/wiki/1994_Cleveland_Indians_corked_bat_incident)

185.

The Evergreen State College mascot is Speedy the Geoduck, a large, saltwater clam that happens to look like a penis.

Reference: (http://www.evergreen.edu/geoduck)

186.

Chang and Eng Bunker, the original Siamese twins, were slave owners in North Carolina whose sons fought in the Confederate Army.

Reference: (https://en.wikipedia.org/wiki/Chang_and_Eng_Bunker#Life)

187.

The term "b-movie" came from 1950s double features and is a reference to the second, usually worse, of the two films shown.

Reference: (https://en.wikipedia.org/wiki/B_movie)

188.

The lyrics in the song "Louie Louie" by the Kingsmen were so difficult to understand that the FBI was asked to investigate for obscenities. No lyrics were ever officially published, and after two years of investigation, the FBI concluded that they were unintelligible.

Reference:(http://www.slate.com/blogs/lexicon_valley/2016/06/27/a_history_of_swearing_in_music.html)

189.

The U.S. area code "321", as in a countdown, is assigned to Brevard County, Florida. Brevard County is home to NASA, the Kennedy Space Center, Space X and Blue Origin. It was re-registered in 1999.

Reference: (https://en.wikipedia.org/wiki/Brevard_County,_Florida)

190.

The first psychiatric ward was established in 705CE Baghdad, Iraq by Al-Razi. Al-Razi also believed that mental disorders should be treated using psychotherapy and drug treatments.

Reference: (https://www.ncbi.nlm.nih.gov/pmc/articles/PMC3705684/#!po=11.9718)

191.

The killer whale is a natural predator of the moose.

Reference: (https://en.wikipedia.org/wiki/Moose#Natural_predators)

192.

Surgeons listen to music while performing surgery.

Reference: (http://www.huffingtonpost.ca/entry/music-surgery_n_6310842)

193.

Roger Ebert panned the popular Brooke Shields' film "The Blue Lagoon" in 1980, claiming, "It made me itch".

Reference: (https://en.wikipedia.org/wiki/The_Blue_Lagoon_(1980_film))

194.

Ronald Reagan's deterioration from Alzheimer's got so bad he once took a mini ceramic White House model out of his fish tank and when asked what he thought it was he answered, "I don't know, but it's something to do with me."

Reference:(https://www.youtube.com/watch?v=GgKC_Se1xaA&feature=youtu.be&t=1h34m44s)

195.

Fruit juice is nutritionally about the same as drinking the same amount of Coca Cola or other soft drinks; for example, 12 ounces of apple juice contains 40 grams of sugar compared to Coke's 39 grams.

Reference: (https://www.healthline.com/nutrition/fruit-juice-is-just-as-bad-as-soda#section4)

196.

Cesar Millan, also known as the "Dog Whisperer," had Jada Smith, wife of Will Smith, as one of his first clients. She was so satisfied that she paid for one year of English tutoring so he can be aired on U.S. television.

Reference: (https://www.cesarsway.com/cesar-millan/cesars-life/about-cesar)

197.

20 days before John F. Kennedy's assassination, the Prime Minister of the Republic of Vietnam was himself assassinated in a CIA-backed coup. Both of their successors would be defined by their failed alliance in the Vietnam War.

Reference: (https://en.wikipedia.org/wiki/Ngo_Dinh_Diem)

198.

Weird Al Yankovic got permission to parody Nickelback, but was unable to make it work and dropped it.

Reference: (https://en.wikipedia.org/wiki/Straight_Outta_Lynwood#Unused_ideas)

199.

An Indian King in 1920 bought 7 Rolls-Royce cars to collect garbage after being denied a test drive in England.

Reference: (https://www.motoroids.com/features/must-read-how-maharaja-of-alwar-took-revenge-on-rolls-royce-by-turning-them-into-garbage-collectors/)

200.

Fahrenheit and Celsius are the same at -40°.

Reference: (http://www.physlink.com/education/AskExperts/ae51.cfm)

201.

Norman Greenbaum, artist of "Spirit in the Sky," is actually Jewish. He was watching TV one night when he came across a country gospel star, thought it looked easy, and wrote his one hit wonder in 15 minutes. This Jewish artist's song about Jesus sold 2 million copies in a year.

Reference:(http://www.nytimes.com/2006/12/24/fashion/24norman.html?referer=https://www.google.com/)

202.

Switzerland does not have an official capital.

Reference: (https://en.wikipedia.org/wiki/Switzerland)

203.

The Twin Paradox states that a twin who left Earth to travel in space would return home to find that their twin has aged more than they have.

Reference: (https://en.wikipedia.org/wiki/Twin_paradox)

204.

Frédéric Auguste Bartholdi, the architect of the Statue of Liberty, enlisted Gustave Eiffel's help to create it. Eiffel would later go on to create the tower in Paris named after him.

Reference: (https://mashable.com/2015/08/05/statue-of-liberty-construction/#Ic8yf3Re0uqm)

205.

Frankie Muniz suffers from long term memory loss and doesn't even remember being on "Malcolm in the Middle."

Reference: (http://ew.com/tv/2017/10/12/frankie-muniz-memory-loss/)

206.

Animals, especially bears, are attracted to railway tracks because of spilled grain and many are killed because of it.

Reference: (http://onlinelibrary.wiley.com/doi/10.1111/acv.12336/abstract)

207.

The song "Who Let the Dogs Out?" by the Baha Men is actually a cover of a song called "Doggie" written by Anslem Douglas.

Reference: (https://en.wikipedia.org/wiki/Who_Let_the_Dogs_Out%3F)

208.

Upon learning that Merrill Lynch was shorting his company's stock, Clarence Saunders responded by trying to buy up all outstanding stock, which would force Merrill Lynch to close their positions at whatever price he demanded. However, the NYSE intervened in Merrill Lynch's favor.

Reference: (https://www.globalfinancialdata.com/gfdblog/?p=3338)

209.

There were a number of Civil War battles in the Arizona Territory, including the Battle of Stanwix Station and the First Battle of Dragoon Springs, which is the only known combat deaths in the modern confines of Arizona.

Reference: (https://en.wikipedia.org/wiki/Confederate_Arizona#Major_campaigns)

210.

Quisp vs. Quake, the characters in the "breakfast feud" between cereals from outer and inner space, were created by Ward and Scott of Rocky and Bullwinkle fame. They also created the Cap'n Crunch character.

Reference: (http://nightflight.com/quisp-vs-quake-the-breakfast-feud-between-cereals-from-outer-and-inner-space/)

211.

An asteroid entered our solar system in 2017, making it the first known interstellar object to pass through the solar system.

Reference: (https://en.wikipedia.org/wiki/%CA%BBOumuamua)

212.

The NBA and the Shanghai Film Group Corporation created a joint venture movie that featured NBA players Dwight Howard, Scottie Pippen, and Carmelo Anthony.

Reference: (https://en.wikipedia.org/wiki/Amazing_(film))

213.

In August 1951, Pont-Saint-Espirit, a small village in France, over 250 people were plagued with an unknown sickness. Some ended up in asylums, and 7 others died. The culprit was later believed to be a bad batch of flour

Reference: (http://www.tootlafrance.ie/features/the-idyllic-french-village-that-went-insane)

214.

Starfish don't have brains or blood.

Reference: (http://www.whalefacts.org/starfish-facts/)

215.

Soviet Russia built a network of nuclear-powered lighthouses, autonomously turning on and off its lights depending on time of year, and broadcasting radio signals to passing ships in the Arctic Circle.

Reference: (http://www.technovelgy.com/ct/Science-Fiction-News.asp?NewsNum=3926)

216.

Jennifer Anniston was reading a magazine with Angelina Jolie on the cover in the movie "The Break Up" after her break up with Brad Pitt.

Reference: (http://www.famousfix.com/topic/the-break-up/trivia)

217.

Bretschneider's formula is an equation for finding the area of any quadrilateral.

Reference: (https://en.wikipedia.org/wiki/Bretschneider%27s_formula)

218.

Not being able to defecate in a public toilet is a condition called parcopresis.

Reference: (https://en.wikipedia.org/wiki/Parcopresis)

219.

An American man had hiccups for 68 years. He was entered in the Guinness World Records.

Reference: (https://en.wikipedia.org/wiki/Hiccup#Society_and_culture)

220.

After the release of the 1974 movie "The Taking of Pelham One Two Three", which involves the hijacking of a New York City subway train that departed at 1:23 PM, the MTA continues to avoid scheduling Manhattan-bound trains to depart at 1:23 out of superstition.

Reference:(https://en.wikipedia.org/wiki/Pelham_Bay_Park_(IRT_Pelham_Line)#The_Taking_of_Pelham_One_Two_Three_superstition)

221.

"Kansas" and "Arkansas" are pronounced differently because the French version of Arkansas, "Arcansas" was used as opposed to others.

Reference:(http://www.slate.com/blogs/lexicon_valley/2014/08/27/why_the_state_names_of_arkansas_and_kansas_are_pronounced_differently.html)

222.

Tom Hanks' younger brother, Jim, sounds so similar to Tom that he often does substitute voice-over work for computer games when Tom doesn't have the time.

Reference: (https://en.wikipedia.org/wiki/Jim_Hanks)

223.

The "Frozen Dead Guy Days" is a festival held in Nederland, Colorado. The festival celebrates the 1994 discovery of the cryonic state corpse of Bredo Morstoel. Morstoel has been and still is to this day cryogenically frozen in a shed within the town.

Reference: (https://en.wikipedia.org/wiki/Frozen_Dead_Guy_Days)

224.

The Square Kilometer Array is a global radio telescope array being built that will produce more than 160 Terabytes of data per second, more than 10 times today's global internet traffic.

Reference: (https://www.skatelescope.org/)

225.

Charlie and Michael Sheen once beat Michael Jordan on the basketball court.

Reference: (https://www.youtube.com/watch?v=JQhRklAIqa0&feature=youtu.be)

226.

The capsule in the middle of a Kinder Surprise Egg is yellow as to represent the yolk of an egg.

Reference: (https://www.joe.co.uk/food/reason-toy-capsule-kinder-eggs-yellow-114990)

227.

Moonbow is a rainbow produced by moonlight rather than sunlight.

Reference: (https://en.wikipedia.org/wiki/Moonbow)

228.

Daniel Radcliffe's stunt double was paralyzed by an injury filming a stunt in the "Harry Potter: The Deathly Hallows."

Reference: (https://www.mirror.co.uk/news/real-life-stories/harry-potter-stuntman-david-holmes-3279214)

229.

Kangaroos and koalas have 3 vaginas.

Reference: (https://gizmodo.com/kangaroos-and-koalas-have-three-vaginas-1605613185)

230.

Archimedes died in the invasion of Syracuse when he angered a Roman soldier. The soldier had told Archimedes to follow the general Marcellus, but Archimedes was so engrossed in his work that he told the soldier "no." The soldier stabbed him with a sword.

Reference: (http://www.livius.org/sources/content/plutarch/plutarchs-marcellus/the-death-of-archimedes/)

231.

Lin-Manuel Miranda's first director in high school was MSNBC host Chris Hayes.

Reference: (http://www.playbill.com/article/which-msnbc-host-directed-lin-manuel-miranda-in-his-first-musical)

232.

A painting resembling Mickey Mouse was found in a 14th century fresco in a church in Austria in 2002.

Reference: (http://news.bbc.co.uk/cbbcnews/hi/world/newsid_2481000/2481511.stm)

233.

In the 1960s, the United States designed a practical plasma weapon for a space battleship.

Reference: (http://www.projectrho.com/public_html/rocket/spacegunconvent.php#id--Nukes_In_Space--Nuclear_Shaped_Charges)

234.

In the 1980s, 53 percent of female coal miners said they had been propositioned by their male bosses and 17 percent said they had been physically attacked.

Reference: (https://www.nytimes.com/1982/10/11/us/women-in-mines-fight-to-be-accepted.html)

235.

Right-handed users of quill pens would use feathers from the left wing, and vice versa.

Reference: (https://en.wikipedia.org/wiki/Quill)

236.

In 2001, rapper Da Brat was given probation for hitting a woman with a rum bottle, and 6 years later sent to prison for hitting a woman with a rum bottle.

Reference: (https://en.wikipedia.org/wiki/Da_Brat#Legal_troubles_and_prison_sentence)

237.

Cashew nuts grow from the bottom end of a fruit called "cashew apples."

Reference: (http://news.sweetandsavory.co/certain-food-grown/?utm_source=page_jb&utm_medium=facebook&utm_campaign=food)

238.

The lyrics to "Turn! Turn! Turn!" by The Byrds are taken almost verbatim from the book of Ecclesiastes, as found in the King James Version of the Bible, though the sequence of the words was rearranged for the song.

Reference: (https://en.wikipedia.org/wiki/Turn!_Turn!_Turn!#Lyrics_and_title)

239.

The Black Swan Project was a U.S. salvage company that tried to secretly steal $500,000 worth of gold from Spanish shipwrecks. The U.S. Supreme Court eventually told them to give Spain back their gold.

Reference: (https://en.wikipedia.org/wiki/Black_Swan_Project)

240.

That St. Edmund is buried in Bury St. Edmunds, U.K.

Reference: (https://en.wikipedia.org/wiki/Edmund_the_Martyr#Memorial_coinage)

241.

As a result of military bombings by the Mexican government starting in the 1900s, a gorgeous "hidden beach" has formed in the Marietta Islands.

Reference: (https://www.thescottishsun.co.uk/living/525992/this-secret-beach-in-mexico-is-completely-hidden-from-prying-eyes/)

242.

The largest cemetery in the world is located in Iraq. It contains over 5 million bodies and spans across 1,485.5 acres.

Reference: (http://valleyofpeaceus.com/Wadi-Us-Salaam.html)

243.

The universe is not expanding but stretching.

Reference: (http://curious.astro.cornell.edu/privacy-policy/104-the-universe/cosmology-and-the-big-bang/expansion-of-the-universe/623-what-is-the-universe-expanding-into-intermediate)

244.

The lowest zip code in the United States is in Holtsville, New York, 00501, and is unique for the IRS servicing center there.

Reference: (http://www.zipboundary.com/zipcode_history.html)

245.

The croissant is not really French. It was inspired by the Austrian kipfel that dates back to at least 1227.

Reference: (https://www.smithsonianmag.com/arts-culture/croissant-really-french-180955130/)

246.

Magic Earring Ken became one of the best-selling Ken dolls of all time.

Reference: (https://money.howstuffworks.com/barbie-earring-magic-ken-gay-icon-1993.htm)

247.

Japan used to have variable-length hours. Six for the day and six for the night, they changed length depending on the season.

Reference: (https://youtu.be/1moRfIXCfak?t=889)

248.

The last royal ceremony in France took place in 2004 when the heart of King Louis XVII was buried next to his parents. It was the first time in over a century that a genuine royal ceremony was held in France.

Reference: (https://en.wikipedia.org/wiki/Louis_XVII_of_France#Heart_of_Louis-Charles)

249.

The largest high school arson in the United States occurred in Burnsville, Minnesota.

Reference: (https://en.wikipedia.org/wiki/Burnsville_High_School)

250.

In order to circumvent laws banning the advertisement of alcohol, the Russian Standard brand of vodka opened the Russian Standard Bank, which has now gone on to become one of the leading banks in the country, with a distribution network covering 93% of the population.

Reference: (https://en.wikipedia.org/wiki/Russian_Standard_Bank)

251.

Most vodkas in the U.S. are pretty much the same, with no distinctive character, aroma, taste, or color.

Reference: (https://www.law.cornell.edu/cfr/text/27/5.22)

252.

The CIA declassified German recipes for invisible ink.

Reference: (https://www.cia.gov/library/readingroom/docs/CIA-RDP11X00001R000100010006-4.pdf)

253.

Amanda Feilding, a British woman, in the 1970s, drilled a hole in her own skull believing that it expands your consciousness and enhances the effects of psychedelics. It was an ancient practice called "trepanation".

Reference: (https://blogs.scientificamerican.com/cross-check/can-a-hole-in-your-head-get-you-high/)

254.

In 1990, the grand marshal of the Los Angeles Gay Pride Parade was an 82 year old retired straight female professor. Her research in the 1950s led to homosexuality no longer being considered a mental illness in the United States.

Reference: (http://articles.latimes.com/1990-06-10/magazine/tm-539_1_gay-liberation)

255.

Admiral John Byng was executed by firing squad for failing to "do his utmost" during the Battle of Minorca at the start of the Seven Years' War.

Reference: (https://en.wikipedia.org/wiki/John_Byng)

256.

You should not get in and out of your vehicle while refueling gas. A static electric charge can develop on your body as you slide across the seat, and when you reach for the pump, a spark can ignite gasoline vapor.

Reference: (https://www.nfpa.org/Public-Education/By-topic/Property-type-and-vehicles/Vehicles/Service-station-safety)

257.

United Airlines has repeatedly killed more pets per year than any other U.S. airline.

Reference: (http://www.latimes.com/opinion/opinion-la/la-ol-united-pet-deaths-20170413-story.html)

258.

Seventh Day Adventists subjected themselves to deadly viruses and bacteria to test the effects of weapons instead of going to war.

Reference: (http://www.pbs.org/wnet/religionandethics/2003/10/24/october-24-2003-operation-whitecoat/15055/)

259.

Ashton Kutcher ended up in the hospital with pancreatic issues after following Steve Jobs' fruitarian diet in preparation for the movie "Jobs." Steve Jobs died of pancreatic cancer.

Reference: (https://www.theguardian.com/film/2013/jan/28/ashton-kutcher-hospital-steve-jobs-diet)

260.

The "Curse of the Pharaoh" theory in biology states that parasites and diseases that can lie dormant for longer tend to be more virulent. The theory is used to explain some untimely deaths of persons involved in the excavation of King Tut's tomb.

Reference: (https://www.nature.com/news/1998/980827/full/news980827-8.html)

261.

Hawaii had a 2017 surge in Spam theft that local retailers believe was perpetrated by organized crime.

Reference: (https://en.wikipedia.org/wiki/Spam_(food))

262.

Wild Bill Hickock's childhood was spent with his family aiding the Underground Railroad helping slaves escape to Canada, this gave him inspiration to find adventures in the west.

Reference: (https://www.britannica.com/biography/Wild-)

263.

Female snakes and lizards can store multiple sources of sperm, choosing which one fertilizes their eggs. They can even take genetic traits from multiple sources, affecting a single clutch of eggs.

Reference: (https://en.wikipedia.org/wiki/Hemipenis#Cryptic_female_choice)

264.

Fidel Castro had a strange dairy obsession, and would craft elaborate schemes such as a "race of super cows" and tiny cows to keep as house pets. He even bred a cow that produced over 100 liters of milk in a day.

Reference: (https://warisboring.com/fidel-castro-had-a-bizarre-obsession-with-milk/)

265.

The University of Colorado named their cafeteria grill after an infamous confessed cannibal, Alferd G. Packer, with the slogan being, "Have a friend for lunch!"

Reference: (https://en.wikipedia.org/wiki/Alferd_Packer)

266.

The Beastie Boy's 1989 album "Paul's Boutique" samples 105 different songs, with 24 sampled on the last track alone.

Reference: (https://en.wikipedia.org/wiki/Paul's_Boutique)

267.

Jack Nicholson banned all Celtics gear from the set of "The Departed".

Reference: (https://www.yahoo.com/news/jack-nicholson-banned-celtics-gear-170823591.html)

268.

The U.S. Postal Service does not have an official motto. The motto generally attributed to it, "Neither snow nor rain nor heat nor gloom of night ...", is a passage from The Persian Wars by Herodotus.

Reference: (https://about.usps.com/who-we-are/postal-history/mission-motto.pdf)

269.

On Christmas 1969, Francisco Macias Nguema executed 150 people with soldiers dressed as Santa Clause while, "Those Were the Days, My Friend", by Mary Hopkin played in the background.

Reference: (https://sites.tufts.edu/atrocityendings/2015/08/07/equatorial-guinea/#_ednref26)

270.

Director Steven Soderbergh was nominated for three Emmys under three different names for "Behind the Candelabra," using the pseudonyms Peter Andrews as cinematographer and Mary Ann Bernard as editor.

Reference:(http://www.slate.com/blogs/browbeat/2013/07/18/steven_soderbergh_and_his_pseudonyms_get_three_2013_emmy_nominations.html)

271.

When male honey bees mate, their penises explode and they die. During the queen's nuptial flight, she'll mate with about a dozen partners and leave a trail of their dead, penisless corpses in her wake.

Reference: (https://owlcation.com/stem/The-Life-of-the-Queen-Bee-in-the-Honey-Bee-Hive)

272.

Certain small aircraft have a whole aircraft parachute system.

Reference: (https://en.wikipedia.org/wiki/Cirrus_Airframe_Parachute_System)

273.

Thomas Marshall, the vice-president under Woodrow Wilson, sat on the lap of Abraham Lincoln during the historic 1858 Lincoln Douglas Debate in Freeport, Illinois.

Reference: (https://en.wikipedia.org/wiki/Thomas_R._Marshall#Family_and_background)

274.

Jailed Nixon advisers John Ehrlichman and J.R. Haldeman were both Christian scientists and they inserted language exempting, "prayer is the only cure", parents from the Child Abuse Prevention and Treatment Act.

Reference: (https://www.theguardian.com/us-news/2016/apr/13/followers-of-christ-idaho-religious-sect-child-mortality-refusing-medical-help)

275.

Kid Rock took a massive pay cut on his 2013 Summer tour in order to keep ticket prices for his shows capped at $20, and beer prices at $4 for 12 ounces.

Reference: (https://www.billboard.com/articles/news/1556609/kid-rock-takes-pay-cut-with-20-tickets-on-summer-tour)

276.

There are goats that have had spider genes mixed with their DNA so their milk produces spider silk.

Reference: (http://www.bbc.com/news/av/science-environment-16554357/the-goats-with-spider-genes-and-silk-in-their-milk)

277.

Three horses, Secretariat, Man o' War, and Citation, are included on ESPN's Top North American Athletes of the Century list.

Reference: (https://www.espn.com/sportscentury/athletes.html)

278.

The Old English Bulldog, the ancestor to the Pit Bull, was used in a sport known as bull baiting, where one or two bulldogs would harass a bull for public entertainment.

Reference: (http://love-a-bull.org/resources/the-history-of-pit-bulls/)

279.

The capital city of the British Overseas Territory of Montserrat is a ghost town.

Reference: (https://en.wikipedia.org/wiki/Plymouth,_Montserrat)

280.

Project Mogul was a U.S. Airforce secret project to detect nuclear tests acoustically with microphones mounted on high altitude balloons. When one such balloon crashed in Roswell, New Mexico in 1947, they covered it up by saying it was a weather balloon.

Reference: (https://en.wikipedia.org/wiki/Project_Mogul)

281.

British entertainer Roy Castle once set a world record by playing the same tune on 43 different instruments in four minutes while Anton Newcombe, front man for The Brian Jonestown Massacre, has claimed to be able to play 80 different instruments.

Reference: (https://en.wikipedia.org/wiki/Multi-instrumentalist#Examples)

282.

Porn star Sunny Lane's career is managed by her parents with whom she lives with in an apartment.

Reference: (https://en.wikipedia.org/wiki/Sunny_Lane?A)

283.

Operation Vegetarian was a British World War II plan to decimate Germany with anthrax laced cakes that would have been fed to cattle. The project was canceled after the test area was devastated and remained a no-go zone until 1990.

Reference: (https://en.wikipedia.org/wiki/Operation_Vegetarian)

284.

The reason why most radio stations begin with a "K" or a "W" is because in the early 1900's, U.S. ships in the Atlantic got three letter call signs starting with a K, and ships in the Pacific got a W prefix to minimize confusion when communicating.

Reference: (http://mentalfloss.com/article/29669/why-do-some-radio-stations-begin-k-and-others-w)

285.

France had a "proto-internet" called Minitel, to which half the population had access. It allowed for buying plane tickets, shopping, 24-hour news, message boards and adult chat services. It was used to coordinate a national strike in 1986. Some believe it hindered the internet's adoption in France.

Reference: (https://en.wikipedia.org/wiki/Minitel)

286.

In the final stages of hypothermia, humans exhibit two strange behaviors; paradoxical undressing, in which a person will remove all their clothes despite being dangerously close to death, and a completely autonomous, instinctual burrowing behavior.

Reference: (https://www.ncbi.nlm.nih.gov/m/pubmed/7632602/)

287.

It has been over six years since the last assassination of a head of state. The previous longest stretch was 1923 to 1932.

Reference:(https://en.wikipedia.org/wiki/List_of_assassinated_and_executed_heads_of_state_and_government)

288.

The Japanese have a contrasting set of words for the true feelings one has deep down, and the behavior projected as a front that conforms to societal norms, that one can switch between in private and public settings.

Reference: (https://en.wikipedia.org/wiki/Honne_and_tatemae)

289.

Starting from the second crusade many in Christendom believed in a powerful Indian Christian King named Prestor John who was about to come with his powerful army from the east to crush the Muslim armies.

Reference: (https://en.wikipedia.org/wiki/Prester_John)

290.

38 Dakota warriors were ordered to be hung by Abraham Lincoln. It was the largest mass execution in U.S. history.

Reference: (http://usdakotawar.org/history/aftermath/trials-hanging)

291.

Flexitarianism, or Semi-Vegetarianism, is a movement trying to encourage people to eat more plant based diets without going on a strict anti-meat diet.

Reference: (https://en.wikipedia.org/wiki/Semi-vegetarianism)

292.

In Japan, male students can confess their love to another person by giving them the second button from the top of their school uniform. The second button is the one closest to the heart.

Reference: (https://en.wikipedia.org/wiki/Japanese_school_uniform)

293.

A 7 year old boy found a giant prehistoric Megalodon shark tooth at Myrtle Beach, South Carolina.

Reference: (https://www.sacbee.com/news/nation-world/national/article163185228.html)

294.

The trap or "bend" in pipes is used to block off hazardous gasses from entering buildings.

Reference: (https://en.wikipedia.org/wiki/Trap_(plumbing))

295.

Women are born with most of their eggs, so there is a good chance that when giving birth to daughters, moms also briefly have part of their grandchildren in them as well.

Reference: (https://www.webmd.com/infertility-and-reproduction/news/20040310/women-not-born-lifetime-eggs#1)

296.

New York Times' puzzle editor Will Shortz designed his own major program at Indiana University, and in 1974 became the first and only holder of a degree in Enigmatology, the study of puzzles.

Reference: (http://willshortz.com/)

297.

Stalin was never officially head of state of the USSR.

Reference:(https://en.wikipedia.org/wiki/List_of_heads_of_state_of_the_Soviet_Union#List_of_heads_of_state)

298.

The Tarahumara Indians from Mexico said that 50 parents had killed themselves because they were not able to feed their children just to call the attention of the media to show the starvation they were suffering.

Reference: (http://articles.latimes.com/2012/jan/18/world/la-fg-mexico-indians-hunger-20120119)

299.

Depictions of knights fighting snails were common in medieval texts. No one really knows why.

Reference: (https://www.smithsonianmag.com/smart-news/why-were-medieval-knights-always-fighting-snails-1728888/)

300.

Friedrich Nietzsche was a composer of music, not just an existential philosopher.

Reference: (https://www.newyorker.com/books/page-turner/nietzsche-was-a-composer-and-not-just-of-books)

301.

Flin Flon, Manitoba, Canada was named after a random pulp science fiction hero the founder just happened to like.

Reference: (https://www.youtube.com/watch?v=vnNDBe48eh8&feature=youtu.be)

302.

Michael Jackson's "Thriller" went platinum not once, not twice, but thirty-three times.

Reference: (https://www.riaa.com/gold-platinum/?tab_active=top_tallies&ttt=DA#search_section)

303.

The Bear Mountain Compact is an unofficial agreement among members of the New York State legislature in which they agree to keep whatever happens in the state capital in Albany, such as extramarital affairs and other embarrassing behaviors or secrets.

Reference: (https://en.wikipedia.org/wiki/Bear_Mountain_Compact)

304.

So many Purple Hearts were produced in the anticipation of the invasion of the Japanese mainland in World War II that they are still being issued today in Iraq and Afghanistan.

Reference: (https://historynewsnetwork.org/article/1801)

305.

Charles Bronson, tough guy actor of classic films like "The Magnificent Seven" and "Death Wish," grew up in abject poverty, the 11th of 15 kids. His family was so poor that he once had to wear his sister's dress to school. When he was 16, he mined coal for $1 per ton.

Reference: (http://www.nytimes.com/2003/09/01/nyregion/charles-bronson-81-dies-muscular-movie-tough-guy.html)

306.

A unit of measurement called micromort is a one-in-a-million chance of death.

Reference: (https://theconversation.com/whats-most-likely-to-kill-you-measuring-how-deadly-our-daily-activities-are-72505)

307.

Bulimia is so rare outside of western countries that the first recorded case in India resulted in a scientific publication.

Reference: (https://www.ncbi.nlm.nih.gov/pmc/articles/PMC3821212/)

308.

Americans between 50 and 64 years old have lost an average of about 10 teeth.

Reference: (https://www.nidcr.nih.gov/research/data-statistics/tooth-loss/adults)

309.

Benjamin Franklin was a fashion icon in France. When he passed away, the French National Assembly declared a day of mourning.

Reference: (https://constitutioncenter.org/blog/americas-first-rock-star-benjamin-franklin-in-france)

310.

David Ogden Stiers, whose character on "M*A*S*H" was a fan of classical music, was an associate conductor as well as guest-conducted over 70 orchestras around the world.

Reference: (https://en.wikipedia.org/wiki/David_Ogden_Stiers)

311.

Lāhainā Noon is a phenomenon that only one state in the U.S. experiences: Hawaii. During this brief period of time, the Sun is directly overhead and objects that stand straight up, like flagpoles, telephone poles, etc., cast no shadow.

Reference: (https://en.wikipedia.org/wiki/Lahaina_Noon)

312.

The word "grenade" comes from the French word for pomegranate whose outer appearance and seeds resemble a grenade and its fragments.

Reference: (https://en.wikipedia.org/wiki/Grenade#Etymology)

313.

The Clash's "London Calling" album artwork copies Elvis' debut album artwork.

Reference: (http://teamrock.com/feature/2016-12-04/the-story-behind-the-clashs-london-calling-album-artwork)

314.

Jackie Bibby set 5 Guinness World Records, all involving snakes. Two of the records were lying in a sleeping bag with the most rattlesnakes and going head first into a sleeping bag with the most rattlesnakes.

Reference: (http://www.texsnakeman.com/)

315.

People used to believe that male possums mated with the female's nose then she sneezed the babies into her marsupial pouch.

Reference: (http://opossumsocietyus.org/general-opossum-information/opossum-reproduction-lifecycle/)

316.

In the early 1900s, San Francisco's Fillmore district had a large Japanese population, until internment during World War II. That, combined with an influx of African Americans taking shipyard work and moving into the vacant homes led to the area becoming the jazz center that it is famed for.

Reference: (https://en.wikipedia.org/wiki/Fillmore_District,_San_Francisco)

317.

São Paulo, a city in Brazil, once tried to elect a rhinoceros with 100,000 votes.

Reference: (https://en.wikipedia.org/wiki/Cacareco)

318.

In the Japanese concept of "Wa", all people strive to put the betterment of the overall society above that of the individual. It is considered an integral part of Japanese society.

Reference: (https://en.wikipedia.org/wiki/Wa_(Japanese_culture))

319.

Archimedes estimated the value of pi with a polygon in a circle in a polygon. He made the diameter of the circle 1, so the circumference was pi. With the circle's diameter, he found the perimeters of the polygons. Therefore, the value of pi, the circle's circumference, is in between them.

Reference: (http://www.businessinsider.com/archimedes-pi-estimation-2014-3)

320.

Golden State Warriors coach Steve Kerr was born in Beirut, Lebanon, where his father taught at the American University of Beirut. In 1982, his father was appointed president of that university, but would be murdered by an Islamic jihadist in 1984.

Reference: (https://en.wikipedia.org/wiki/Steve_Kerr#Early_life)

321.

While filming a scene in the live action "Jungle Book" where Mowgli meets King Louie, who is played by Christopher Walken, director Jon Favreau spotted a cowbell on stage and said, "This is what Mowgli has to use." Mowgli rings the bell to awaken Louie as an homage to Christopher Walken's Saturday Night Live skit.

Reference: (https://www.moviefone.com/2016/04/12/disney-live-action-jungle-book-jon-favreau-interview/)

322.

In the ocean's Deep Sound Channel, the phenomenon of refraction allows sound to travel for thousands of miles.

Reference: (https://en.wikipedia.org/wiki/SOFAR_channel)

323.

The largest indoor ropes course is inside a furniture store.

Reference: (http://www.courant.com/news/connecticut/hc-jordans-furniture-opens-in-new-haven-20151210-story.html)

324.

The black and white striped prison uniform began in an Auburn prison, in Auburn, New York.

Reference: (https://en.wikipedia.org/wiki/Auburn_Correctional_Facility)

325.

The first parking ticket in London wasn't issued until 1960.

Reference: (https://www.telegraph.co.uk/motoring/news/8087984/50-years-of-traffic-wardens.html)

326.

The Tichborne Dole is a charitable giveaway of flour started by a dying matriarch in the 12th century.

Reference: (https://en.wikipedia.org/wiki/Tichborne_Dole)

327.

When a shark is flipped on its back it enters a state of paralysis that lasts for up to fifteen minutes. The phenomenon is known as "Tonic Immobility." In some cases, orcas have been seen maneuvering a shark upside down to induce this paralyzed state.

Reference: (http://animals.mom.me/causes-shark-slide-trance-upside-down-11121.html)

328.

Before someone figured out how to teach a horse to fall down for a movie, hundreds were deliberately tripped-up or made to fall into traps and then killed if they became injured.

Reference: (https://www.telegraph.co.uk/films/ben-hur/hollywood-horse-trainer/)

329.

Jayne Mansfield, Carroll O'Connor, Jerry Van Dyke, and Raquel Welch were all nearly cast on Gilligan's Island as Ginger, the Skipper, Gilligan, and Mary Ann.

Reference: (https://www.metv.com/lists/8-actors-who-were-almost-cast-on-gilligans-island)

330.

There is a gene that can cause your breasts to shrink if you consume too much caffeine.

Reference: (https://www.snpedia.com/index.php/Rs762551(C;C))

331.

Harvey Fierstein's voice is so famously gravely because he was in a play called "Xircus, The Private Life of Jesus Christ" and had to do a 5 page monologue over a very loud recording of Kate Smith singing "God Bless America." The director refused to turn down the volume, and he wanted every word heard.

Reference: (http://www.donshewey.com/theater_reviews/fiddler_on_the_roof.html)

332.

Elderly koalas usually die of starvation before they are able to reach "old age death". This is because their teeth gradually wear down from chewing until they are no longer functional as a means of grinding food down. The resulting consequence is a very hungry koala.

Reference: (http://koalainfo.com/most-koalas-die-of-starvation)

333.

A "Tontine" is an arrangement where a group of people buy into a lottery, and whoever lives the longest wins the entire pot.

Reference: (https://en.wikipedia.org/wiki/Tontine)

334.

An employer once convinced an administrative law judge to vacate a $238,000 OSHA citation by arguing he was no longer an "employer" when the citation was issued because the accident killed all three of his employees.

Reference: (https://www.necanet.org/about-us/news/news-release-archive/news/1999/04/19/going-out-of-business-no-way-to-beat-osha-citation)

335.

Jeff Skilling, former CEO of Enron, cut a deal with the Department Of Justice that resulted in 10 years being cut from his sentence. He is due to be released in February, 2019.

Reference: (https://www.reuters.com/article/us-enron-skilling/former-enron-ceo-skillings-sentence-cut-to-14-years-idUSBRE95K12520130621)

336.

A rikishi is a professional sumo wrestler.

Reference: (https://en.wikipedia.org/wiki/Rikishi)

337.

Grigori Perelman is a mathematician who in 2003 proved the Poincaré conjecture, a long unsolved problem in mathematics, and later declined the Fields Medal, a $1 million Clay Millennium Prize and other awards.

Reference: (https://en.wikipedia.org/wiki/Grigori_Perelman)

338.

You are born with 270 bones but due to fusing have 206 as an adult.

Reference: (https://en.wikipedia.org/wiki/List_of_bones_of_the_human_skeleton)

339.

One of the first radio communications from an aircraft in flight was, "Roy, come and get this goddamn cat."

Reference: (http://mentalfloss.com/article/49780/kiddo-airborne-cat)

340.

Fashion is excluded from protection of copyright laws.

Reference: (https://en.wikipedia.org/wiki/Fashion_design_copyright)

341.

Our public school system was invented in 19th century Prussia

Reference: (https://www.theatlantic.com/business/archive/2012/05/how-to-break-free-of-our-19th-century-factory-model-education-system/256881/)

342.

A village in India is addicted to chess after one man taught everyone how to play 50 years ago to stop excessive alcohol use and gambling, which has now all declined to almost nothing.

Reference: (http://www.bbc.com/travel/story/20170511-the-indian-village-addicted-to-chess)

343.

While approximately 25 times smaller than Canada, California boasts over 2 million more residents.

Reference: (http://www.mylifeelsewhere.com/country-size-comparison/canada/california-usa)

344.

Meryl Streep, with 21 nominations, is the actress with the most Oscar nominations. This is almost twice the amount of what the actor and actress in the second place have: Katharine Hepburn and Jack Nicholson with 12 nominations each.

Reference: (https://en.wikipedia.org/wiki/List_of_actors_with_Academy_Award_nominations)

345.

Shannon Hoon, the late lead singer of Blind Melon, also sang backup vocals for Guns 'n Roses and appeared in their famous "Don't Cry" music video.

Reference: (https://en.wikipedia.org/wiki/Shannon_Hoon)

346.

Henry Thomas, the child actor in E.T., thought of his dead dog to bring him to tears during his famous audition with Steven Spielberg.

Reference: (https://youtu.be/jiE-nMDFpVA?t=1m5s)

347.

Bernie Madoff's best friend in prison is Carmine John Persico Jr., boss of the Columbo crime family, who is serving more than 100 years in the same prison.

Reference: (https://nypost.com/2017/05/20/bernie-madoffs-closest-prison-pal-is-a-crime-family-boss?iframe=true&theme_preview=true)

348.

To gain and maintain their weight, sumo wrestlers eat a special diet of a stew called chankonabe. Chankonabe is so delicious that after retirement, many Sumo wrestlers start their own restaurants.

Reference: (https://www.tofugu.com/japan/sumo-diet/)

349.

ADT, the security company, originally formed in 1874 as a telegraph-based security company called American District Telegraph, moving away from telegraphs in the 1920s when the technology started to become obsolete. They were also owned by AT&T from 1909 until 1914.

Reference: (https://www.yourlocalsecurity.com/resources/adt-timeline)

350.

The world's first recorded St Patrick's Day celebration was in St. Augustine, Florida, in the year 1600.

Reference:(https://en.wikipedia.org/wiki/Saint_Patrick%27s_Day_in_the_United_States#Early_celebrations)

351.

There are no female leprechauns in Irish folklore.

Reference: (https://www.irishcentral.com/culture/entertainment/top-ten-facts-about-leprechauns-and-where-the-legends-really-came-from-212728761-237598771)

352.

At the Dry Valleys, Antarctica, the driest place on Earth, downward cold winds called katabatic winds can reach 200 miles per hour, or 322 kilometers per hour, evaporating any water, ice or snow.

Reference: (https://en.wikipedia.org/wiki/McMurdo_Dry_Valleys#Climate)

353.

Fuses have sand inside them.

Reference: (http://www.fuseco.com.au/help/faq_low_voltage_fuses/3071?pid=13423&sid=)

354.

Hitler's "Eagle's Nest" on the summit of the Kehlstein Mountain is today a restaurant and outdoor pub.

Reference: (https://en.wikipedia.org/wiki/Kehlsteinhaus#Today)

355.

Pre-made salad has no added preservatives. Instead, each bag is packed using a special mixture of gasses which serve as natural preservatives.

Reference: (http://www.tbo.com/dining/the----on-bagged-salad-mix-301632)

356.

Celebrity chef Alton Brown worked as a cinematographer and video director before he became a food star. He was the director of photography for R.E.M.'s music video "The One I Love" and spent all of his time between takes on the set watching cooking shows, feeling that he could do a better job.

Reference: (https://www.biography.com/people/alton-brown-20914593)

357.

The movies "Temple of Doom" and "Gremlins" led Steven Spielberg to request the MPAA create a rating between PG and R. Consequently, the PG-13 rating was created.

Reference: (https://www.stuffyoushouldknow.com/podcasts/how-the-mpaa-works.htm)

358.

In December, 2015, U-Haul was used by UPS to help temporarily expand UPS's fleet to handle a surge due to Christmas and other holiday volume.

Reference: (https://en.wikipedia.org/wiki/U-Haul#History)

359.

You're more likely to overdose from heroin on a relapse. People who use heroin long enough eventually build up a tolerance. What happens is people who get sober sometimes relapse but take a dose they were on at their worst. They unintentionally kill themselves by not realizing their tolerance dropped.

Reference: (http://www.businessinsider.com/philip-seymour-hoffman-overdose-2014-2)

360.

"Medical Food" is a special category of medical product that may require a prescription, but may not be covered by insurance because it is a "food", yet does not require approval by the FDA.

Reference: (https://en.wikipedia.org/wiki/Medical_food#Regulation)

361.

In English, kilocalorie is also called Calorie, with an uppercase "C", yet both equal to 1000 calories, with a smaller "c".

Reference: (http://www.kirkmahoney.com/blog/2009/01/calorie-vs-calorie/)

362.

Russia hosts over 186 ethnic groups designated as nationalities, making it one of the most culturally diverse nations on the planet.

Reference: (https://en.wikipedia.org/wiki/Ethnic_groups_in_Russia)

363.

Richard Nixon was an accomplished musician who could play piano, accordion, violin, saxophone, and clarinet. He even wrote his own concerto titled "Richard Nixon Piano Concerto #1."

Reference: (http://mentalfloss.com/article/76572/richard-nixons-impromptu-piano-recital)

364.

The Winter Paralympics include a biathlon, for the visually impaired.

Reference: (https://www.disabled-world.com/sports/paralympics/2010/biathlon-skiing-shooting.php)

365.

Promethea Unbound is a child genius brought at age 5 to the Stanford particle accelerator where she stunned the scientists there with her intellect. Her life later became unwound by a horrific act of violence.

Reference: (https://magazine.atavist.com/promethea-unbound-child-genius-montana)

366.

Penn and Teller designed a video game called "Desert Bus" in which the player drove an 8-hour bus route in real time between Tucson and Las Vegas. It is impossible to cheat, the only scenery are rocks and road signs, and once the player reached the destination, they had to turn around and drive back.

Reference: (https://www.newyorker.com/tech/elements/desert-bus-the-very-worst-video-game-ever-created)

367.

The original idea behind the Belcher family in "Bob's Burgers" was that they are cannibals.

Reference: (http://www.businessinsider.com/bobs-burgers-was-originally-about-cannibals-2016-5)

368.

Mike Shinoda, of the group Linkin Park, is a third generation Japanese-American. Some of the artworks he has painted are featured in the Japanese American National Museum.

Reference: (https://en.wikipedia.org/wiki/Japanese_American_National_Museum#Exhibits)

369.

Punjabi is 10th most spoken language in the world.

Reference: (https://www.babbel.com/en/magazine/the-10-most-spoken-languages-in-the-world)

370.

The string of back injuries that ended Larry Bird's career originated from a promise to build his mother a new driveway. In 1985, he built it by himself, injuring his back shoveling gravel in the process.

Reference: (https://youtu.be/axbIoHqFaa8?t=1h7m17s)

371.

The fourth, fifth and sixth time derivatives of position are named Snap, Crackle and Pop.

Reference: (https://en.wikipedia.org/wiki/Snap,_Crackle_and_Pop)

372.

Casimir Pulaski was a Polish nobleman who led a Polish uprising, then immigrated to the U.S. during American Revolutionary War. He died at the age of 34 after attempting to rally fleeing French forces during a cavalry charge, Pulaski was mortally wounded by grapeshot.

Reference: (https://en.wikipedia.org/wiki/Casimir_Pulaski?repost#Death_and_burial)

373.

The martial art Sherlock Holmes used in fighting was baritsu, which is a real mixed martial art.

Reference: (https://en.wikipedia.org/wiki/Bartitsu#"Baritsu"_and_Sherlock_Holmes)

374.

In mushroom related deaths, the Amanita make up of 95% of the fatalities, with 50% of them from the death cap, which is commonly mistaken for edible mushroom varieties. The toxins irreversibly destroy liver cell functions and can require a transplant.

Reference: (https://en.wikipedia.org/wiki/Amanita)

375.

There is a name for when you go driving and deliberately avoid tolls. It's called shunpiking.

Reference: (https://en.wikipedia.org/wiki/Shunpiking)

376.

Jackie Chan has a successful music career.

Reference: (https://en.wikipedia.org/wiki/Jackie_Chan#Music_career)

377.

India has a biometric ID system.

Reference: (https://en.wikipedia.org/wiki/Aadhaar)

378.

Libraries used to keep books chained to the bookcase and shelves during the Middle Ages as books were so valuable. The chaining of books was widely practiced until the 18th century.

Reference: (https://www.smithsonianmag.com/smart-news/libraries-used-to-chain-their-books-to-shelves-with-the-spines-hidden-away-4392158/)

379.

The United States does not have an official language.

Reference: (https://www.usconstitution.net/consttop_lang.html)

380.

Due to its terrible odor, the durian fruit is banned on public transit in Southeast Asia.

Reference: (https://www.smithsonianmag.com/science-nature/why-does-the-durian-fruit-smell-so-terrible-149205532/)

381.

In the 1920s, a man falsely claiming to be a doctor implanted goat testicles into people across the U.S. as a cure for all diseases. He was condemned by the AMA and media, but ran for governor of Kansas in 1930, narrowly losing after thousands of votes for him were questionably disqualified.

Reference: (https://en.wikipedia.org/wiki/John_R._Brinkley)

382.

Chad and Romania have the same flag.

Reference: (https://en.wikipedia.org/wiki/Flag_of_Chad)

383.

The cat in the beginning of "The Godfather" was not in the original script. The director ventured upon the stray in the parking lot and brought it on set.

Reference: (http://www.cinemacats.com/?p=1097)

384.

Cabbage, broccoli, cauliflower, kale, Brussels sprouts, and collard greens are all the same species of plant.

Reference: (https://en.wikipedia.org/wiki/Brassica_oleracea)

385.

The composition of the arthropod head has been one of the most controversial topics in zoology.

Reference: (https://en.wikipedia.org/wiki/Arthropod_head_problem)

386.

The rarest blood type on Earth is RHnull with only 43 people reported on Earth with that blood type.

Reference: (https://www.fastmed.com/health-resources/what-is-the-rarest-blood-type/)

387.

The Canadian military has developed a stealth snowmobile that is able to switch to "silent mode" for covert special ops missions in the Arctic.

Reference: (https://www.popularmechanics.com/technology/infrastructure/a9441/the-secret-stealth-snowmobile-canada-wont-let-you-see-15835701/)

388.

There is a theory in biblical scholarship that Jesus of Nazareth and Pilate's "other" prisoner, Barabbas, were one and the same.

Reference: (https://en.wikipedia.org/wiki/Barabbas)

389.

Singer Barry White was once arrested for stealing $30,000 worth of Cadillac tires.

Reference: (http://news.bbc.co.uk/2/hi/entertainment/2386227.stm)

390.

Ronald Alexander appeared on "The Ellen DeGeneres Show" to accept a $500,000 donation from Lowes for his crumbling elementary school in Detroit. Months later, he and 12 other principals were convicted of taking $900,000 in bribes from a school supply scam.

Reference: (http://www.foxnews.com/us/2016/03/30/thirteen-detroit-school-officials-charged-in-bribery-scheme.html)

391.

In 1901, a doctor was told mid-surgery that he was needed urgently elsewhere, to which he responded that he could not leave, "even for the President of the United States". He was then told he needed to operate on William McKinley, the President of the United States.

Reference: (https://en.wikipedia.org/wiki/Assassination_of_William_McKinley#Operation)

392.

James Hemings is the brother of Sally Hemings and Martha Jefferson. He was one of Thomas Jefferson's slaves that was brought to Paris with Jefferson to have him trained as a classically French trained chef. He introduced ice cream, whipped cream, mac and cheese, French fries, and crème brulee to the U.S.

Reference: (https://www.npr.org/sections/thesalt/2015/10/17/449447335/behind-the-founding-foodie-a-french-trained-chef-bound-by-slavery)

393.

Tatouine, from Star Wars, is a real town in Tunisia, spelled Tataouine, and it's famous for its cave dwellings.

Reference: (https://en.wikipedia.org/wiki/Tataouine)

394.

Trimethylamine, which is the chemical responsible for the fishy smell, binds to the casein in milk. Once washed with water, the remaining product no longer tastes like the sea.

Reference: (https://lifehacker.com/5921337/soak-fish-in-milk-for-odor-free-cooking-and-eating)

395.

John Lennon witnessed a UFO in 1974.

Reference: (https://www.dailystar.co.uk/news/latest-news/540174/john-lennon-ufo-sighting-new-york-revelation-beatles-mary-peng)

396.

When George Washington passed away in 1799, the British Royal Navy lowered its flags at half-mast. The London Morning Chronicle stated that, "The whole range of history does not present to our view a character upon which we can dwell with such entire and unmixed admiration".

Reference: (https://www.historytoday.com/richard-cavendish/death-george-washington)

397.

Family members can buy a smaller version of a Super Bowl ring.

Reference: (http://www.sportscollectorsdigest.com/10-things-you-might-not-know-about-super-bowl-rings/)

398.

If you eat a lot of papaya it will make you to look yellow faster than eating carrots would.

Reference: (https://www.ncbi.nlm.nih.gov/m/pubmed/23931131/)

399.

In 1926, a Danish scientist won the Nobel Prize in medicine for a study in which he fed rats cockroaches that were infected with a species of worm he called Spiroptera neoplastica, wrongly concluding that the worms caused cancer.

Reference: (http://www.slate.com/articles/health_and_science/explainer/2012/10/who_is_the_least_deserving_winner_of_a_nobel_prize_.html)

400.

HIV can be divided into two major types, type 1 and type 2. HIV-1 is found in chimps and gorillas living in West Africa while HIV-2 viruses are found in the endangered West African sooty mangabey. HIV-2 viruses are thought to be less virulent and transmissible than HIV-1 M group viruses.

Reference: (https://en.wikipedia.org/wiki/Subtypes_of_HIV)

401.

The first known image of Stonehenge suggests that Merlin used magic, a giant, and army to help erect the stone formation.

Reference: (http://britishlibrary.typepad.co.uk/digitisedmanuscripts/2014/07/set-in-stone.html)

402.

Molotov cocktails were originally created for use as anti-tank weapons.

Reference: (https://en.wikipedia.org/wiki/Molotov_cocktail)

403.

It is estimated that the world's 25 million tons of spiders kill 400 to 800 million tons of prey per year.

Reference: (https://en.wikipedia.org/wiki/Spider)

404.

Chinese scientists developed a 15 centimeter thick wooden heat shield, made of oak for their FSW recoverable satellite project starting in the 1960's, which was a success.

Reference: (https://www.youtube.com/watch?v=ytZ5jxZOMaE)

405.

Étienne Léopold Trouvelot, in the 1860's, attempted to cross breed gypsy moths and silk worms in his back yard, causing a veracious invasive species that cannot be controlled.

Reference: (https://dotearth.blogs.nytimes.com/2016/07/07/a-war-for-the-woods-as-an-asian-fungus-slightly-blunts-gypsy-moth-outbreaks/)

406.

Male echidna's have a four-headed penis.

Reference: (https://www.menshealth.com/sex-women/weird-penis-animals-humans)

407.

Two weeks before the Castle Gate Mine disaster that killed 171 men, the Utah Fuel Company laid off many of the miners without dependents during a shortage of coal sales. As a result, 114 of the men killed in the disaster were married men and left behind 415 widows and fatherless children.

Reference: (https://en.wikipedia.org/wiki/Castle_Gate_Mine_disaster#Aftermath)

408.

The spotted hyena is to one African tribe what the black cat is in the U.S., owned by witches and used for black magic.

Reference: (http://www.wearesites.com/Personal/Hyenas/hy_folklore.html)

409.

Tarantism is a disease once thought to result from the bite of the tarantula spider. This extraordinary affliction was associated with melancholy, stupor, madness and an uncontrollable desire to dance. In fact, dancing off the tarantula venom was considered the only cure.

Reference: (https://www.medicinenet.com/script/main/art.asp?articlekey=10637)

410.

The only rainbow river in the world occurs between the wet season and dry season in Columbia.

Reference: (https://www.youtube.com/watch?v=cDAIrwGLDdk)

411.

Newly discovered fossils show that moths and butterflies have been on the planet for at least 200 million years, whereas flowering plants came along around 130 million years ago. Butterflies survived without flowers for 70 million years.

Reference: (http://www.newsweek.com/ancient-wing-scale-fossils-re-write-evolutionary-history-moths-and-butterflies-777353)

412.

The Sex Pistols manager's son destroyed nearly $7 million dollars' worth of punk memorabilia.

Reference: (https://www.huffingtonpost.com/entry/sex-pistols-burn-memorabilia_us_583a275ae4b01ba68ac4beae)

413.

Eminem's album The Eminem Show was used by C.I.A. in 2004 to torture a man they held in a secret prison in Afghanistan.

Reference: (https://thelede.blogs.nytimes.com/2009/03/09/claim-us-used-eminem-raps-on-detainees/)

414.

There was a local lore that the color of the nearby Grand Union Canal changed from week to week depending on the activity at William Henry Perkin's Greenford Dyeworks.

Reference: (https://en.wikipedia.org/wiki/William_Henry_Perkin)

415.

The Agora Grand Event Center is the tallest building in Maine, and has been for 130 years.

Reference: (https://en.wikipedia.org/wiki/Agora_Grand_Event_Center)

416.

Monty Python's working title for Life of Brian was, "Jesus Christ: Lust for Glory".

Reference: (https://www.telegraph.co.uk/culture/film/6679546/What-did-Life-of-Brian-ever-do-for-us.html)

417.

40 million year old bones found by paleontologists have revealed a penguin that stood approximately 6 feet, or 2 meters tall, and weighed 220 pounds, or 100 kilograms, and had a hooked beak. Smaller penguins coexisted but the larger species died out.

Reference: (https://www.popsci.com/giant-ancient-penguin#page-3)

418.

After leaving office, Ronald Reagan was offered the role of Hill Valley's mayor in "Back to the Future III."

Reference: (http://ftw.usatoday.com/2015/10/back-to-the-future-facts-about-trilogy-future-day-eric-stoltz-video-trivia-marty-mcfly-spielberg-zemeckis)

419.

According to the U.S. Bureau of Engraving and Printing, it is believed that the origin of the American dollar sign, $, is an evolved version of the symbol for the Mexican Peso, which used to be a "P" and then had the "S" added on-top of it.

Reference: (https://www.moneyfactory.gov/resources/faqs.html)

420.

Upon reaching 65 years old, the monarch of Bhutan must abdicate in favor of the Crown Prince or Crown Princess, provided the royal heir has reached age 21.

Reference: (http://www.constitution.bt/TsaThrim%20Eng%20(A5).pdf)

421.

An estimated 1 million dogs in the U.S. have been named primary beneficiary in their owners' wills.

Reference: (https://www.worldanimalfoundation.com/companions/dogs/)

422.

Cuba wanted to invade Spain during World War II.

Reference: (https://en.wikipedia.org/wiki/Cuba_during_World_War_II)

423.

Kea parrots warble together when they're in a good mood, making them the first known non-mammal species to communicate with infectious laughter.

Reference: (https://www.theatlantic.com/science/archive/2017/03/kea-parrot-laughter-play-hahahahahaha-lolz/520089/)

424.

The majority of deaths from heroin overdose are single men.

Reference: (https://www.cnn.com/2014/02/04/health/how-heroin-kills/index.html)

425.

The pineapple became a sign of hospitality during America's colonial era. The exotic fruit was an expensive treat originally served to only the most-honored guest. Towns, inns and individual households began displaying images of the fruit in order to convey a sense of welcoming.

Reference: (https://www.mnn.com/your-home/at-home/stories/how-pineapple-became-worldwide-symbol-hospitality)

426.

In 1989, 19 boys were tortured, mutilated and castrated by a UFO cult that claimed Jesus was an alien and boys born after 1981 were evil.

Reference: (http://murderpedia.org/male.F/f/ferreira-anisio.htm)

427.

Similarly to "the Netherlands", one should call the African country Gambia as "the Gambia", or "Republic of the Gambia".

Reference: (http://www.ilo.org/dyn/travail/docs/1952/GMB48490.pdf)

428.

Harrison Ford's son invented cauliflower rice.

Reference: (https://www.tastecooking.com/caul-me-by-your-name/)

429.

Tony Lane designed hundreds of record covers, the entire Hollywood Babylon book, and the Kia logo.

Reference: (http://www.printmag.com/design-culture-2/art-director-designer-tony-lane-music-design/)

430.

Super Soaker was bought by Nerf, who no longer produces high water pressure guns.

Reference: (http://www.isoaker.com/Info/2013/01/20130107-when-and-how-did-super-soaker-get-nerfed.html)

431.

Baby snake bites are not more dangerous than adult bites.

Reference: (https://viper.arizona.edu/faq/baby-snakes-are-more-dangerous-adults-right)

432.

Billy Mills won gold at the 1964 Tokyo Olympics, after growing up on the poorest Native American reservation in the United States.

Reference: (https://en.wikipedia.org/wiki/Billy_Mills)

433.

The mayor of Felicity, California, has built a pyramid, a church, a wall, a maze, and a stairway to nowhere because he believes it's the center of the world.

Reference: (https://www.roadsideamerica.com/story/2036)

434.

There is a condition called Hemispatial Neglect where the sufferer can only pay attention to half of whatever they experience. For example, people will only eat half of what is on their plate because they don't know there is a full plate of food in front of them.

Reference: (http://jnnp.bmj.com/content/75/1/13)

435.

George Washington never wore a wig, his hair was naturally long and lustrous. His hairstyle was common among army officers.

Reference: (https://www.smithsonianmag.com/smart-news/how-george-washington-did-his-hair-180955547/)

436.

CD Projekt, developer of "The Witcher" games, started off localizing games to Poland after they could no longer sell pirated games from the west.

Reference: (https://www.youtube.com/watch?v=uNZkTk5gLuo&feature=youtu.be&t=13m19s)

437.

Maroon 5 released a rock album in 1997 under the band name Kara's Flowers. "Soap Disco" was the lead single that never got the light of day.

Reference: (https://www.youtube.com/watch?v=JQXo8uttL34&feature=youtu.be)

438.

Benjamin Franklin had an abusive older brother who forced him to sign an indenture until he was 21 in Boston. His brother was abusive partly because Benjamin showed talent. At age 17, he ran away penniless to Philadelphia, gained connections and jump-started his political career.

Reference: (http://www.benjamin-franklin-history.org/early-life/)

439.

Researchers from Texas State University left a human corpse on a 26-acre woodland site to study how human bodies decompose in the wild. They ended up capturing the first image of a deer eating human remains.

Reference: (https://www.ibtimes.co.uk/see-deer-eating-human-first-time-recorded-history-1620955)

440.

Frederick W. Smith, the CEO, founder and chairman of FedEx, has separately killed two people in motor vehicle accidents: one in a hit and run, for which he was released on $250 bond, and another where he lost control, causing the vehicle to flip, killing the passenger.

Reference:(https://en.wikipedia.org/wiki/Frederick_W._Smith#Forgery_indictment_and_fatal_car_accidents)

441.

The popular sleeping aid known as Ambien, zolpidem tartrate, was astonishingly discovered to bring back some minimally conscious patients back from a vegetative state.

Reference: (http://www.nytimes.com/2011/12/04/magazine/can-ambien-wake-minimally-conscious.html)

442.

Bram Stoker wrote a non-fiction book that claimed that Queen Elizabeth I was really a man.

Reference: (https://www.historyanswers.co.uk/kings-queens/the-virgin-king-was-queen-elizabeth-i-really-a-man/)

443.

Blood from pregnant horses is used in the livestock industry for increasing reproductive rates in pigs.

Reference: (https://www.thedodo.com/turning-horse-blood-into-profits-1382177497.html)

444.

A mother black lace-weaver spider will drum on her web to call her babies to come and eat her alive.

Reference: (https://en.wikipedia.org/wiki/Amaurobius_ferox)

445.

KFC is the leading fast food chain in China and even opened an experimental restaurant focused on fruit juice and salad.

Reference: (http://www.straitstimes.com/lifestyle/food/why-kfc-is-chinas-reigning-fast-food-champion)

446.

The Atlanta Braves are the oldest continually operating franchise in MLB. They were established in January of 1871, less than 6 years after the end of the Civil War.

Reference: (https://www.mlb.com/braves/history/story-of-the-braves)

447.

There is a functioning door in Westminster Abbey that is over 900 years old.

Reference: (http://www.westminster-abbey.org/worship/sermons/2005/august/the-westminster-abbey-anglo-saxon-door)

448.

An earthquake, tsunami, and firestorm hit Lisbon on All Saints' Day in 1755, resulting in the damage of 85% of its buildings and the deaths of thousands.

Reference: (https://www.youtube.com/watch?v=FGhv6zcBPxQ&index=3&list=PL--IcfCujHzlRxgH-VQvyn9gBxLJ7tPR8)

449.

J.K. Rowling thought the casting of Hermione, Ron, and Harry was perfect except for one thing, the actors were too good looking for their geeky characters.

Reference: (https://www.youtube.com/watch?v=7BdVHWz1DPU&feature=youtu.be&t=317)

450.

When Mahatma Gandhi worked in South Africa in his youth, he was exposed to British media reports of New Zealand's Māori people, who set up a village to peacefully resist government occupation of land in the late 1800s. This is thought to have influenced Gandhi's methods of nonviolent resistance.

Reference: (https://en.wikipedia.org/wiki/Te_Whiti_o_Rongomai)

451.

Pope Francis hasn't watched television in almost 30 years after he promised the Virgin Mary that he wouldn't anymore.

Reference: (http://abcnews.go.com/International/wireStory/fun-facts-pope-francis-year-mark-53679070?cid=social_twitter_abcn)

452.

Jimmy Page, when played a song and asked to rate the guitar playing out of 10, gave Muddy Waters a 10, himself an 11, and Steely Dan a 12.

Reference: (https://www.youtube.com/watch?v=wtEXfEwJf4M&feature=youtu.be)

453.

The Vatican has its own list of best movies of all time, featuring titles like: "2001: A Space Odyssey", "Metropolis" and "Schindler's List".

Reference: (https://en.wikipedia.org/wiki/Vatican%27s_list_of_films)

454.

There was a popular series of salsa commercials where the punchline was that they would lynch the cook when discovering that his salsa was from the north.

Reference: (https://www.youtube.com/watch?v=vgrGyR6EYbY)

455.

Stuart Copeland, the drummer with The Police, composed the music for the popular video game, "Spyro the Dragon".

Reference:(https://en.wikipedia.org/wiki/Stewart_Copeland#Spyro_the_Dragon_soundtracks_(1998%E2%80%932002))

456.

A 4-dimensional sphere is called a "Glome".

Reference: (http://mathworld.wolfram.com/Four-DimensionalGeometry.html)

457.

The Superfund Program was created to pay for the cleanup of hazardous waste sites where the polluter was unable to be identified or was unable to pay. Polluters later identified were taken to court, but initial funding for the program came from a tax on chemical and petroleum industries.

Reference: (https://en.wikipedia.org/wiki/Superfund)

458.

At the Civil War's Battle of Shiloh, in 1862, Confederate General Albert Sidney Johnston's leg was struck by a bullet, hitting a major blood vessel, but because of a former nerve injury and his boot hiding the blood, he didn't notice until he bled to death with a tourniquet in his pocket.

Reference: (https://en.wikipedia.org/wiki/Albert_Sidney_Johnston#Battle_of_Shiloh_and_death)

459.

The Great Pyramid of Giza shone bright white when initially built, its limestone slabs polished to reflect the desert Sun.

Reference: (https://www.youtube.com/watch?v=ujX9MEnYzU4&feature=youtu.be)

460.

The New York City Department of Health and researchers from Columbia University monitor foodborne illness outbreaks by using a machine learning computer system which searches Yelp for key words and phrases such as "got sick," "vomit," "diarrhea," and "food poisoning."

Reference: (https://www.atlasobscura.com/articles/food-poisoning-health-yelp)

461.

A self-caused iron deficiency anemia through cutting is called Lasthénie de Ferjol syndrome.

Reference: (https://www.ncbi.nlm.nih.gov/m/pubmed/20575994/)

462.

The Denver Zephyrs minor league baseball team was moved to New Orleans, had a fan vote and was renamed to the New Orleans Baby Cakes in 2017.

Reference:(https://en.wikipedia.org/wiki/New_Orleans_Baby_Cakes#New_Orleans_(1993%E2%80%93present))

463.

Ashley Smith is a Canadian inmate who, despite being placed on suicide watch, was able to strangle herself with a strip of cloth. The incident had a visible impact on Canadian politics in the following years and spawned two judicial inquiries and several documentaries.

Reference: (https://en.wikipedia.org/wiki/Ashley_Smith_inquest)

464.

Some broadcast speed up TV shows by up to 7% to fit more commercials.

Reference: (https://www.youtube.com/watch?v=HzujLPnLg3s)

465.

A bird called the Eurasian Woodcock has a 360 degree field of view.

Reference: (https://www.thainationalparks.com/species/eurasian-woodcock)

466.

Jon "Neverdie" Jacobs mortgaged his home to buy a virtual asteroid for $100,000. In 2005, this was the most valuable virtual item ever sold. This landed him in the Guinness Book of World Records for owning the most expensive virtual item, which he later sold for $635,000.

Reference: (https://en.wikipedia.org/wiki/Jon_Jacobs_(actor))

467.

Sam Raimi, the director of the "Spider-Man" trilogy, actually directed a Spider-Man movie in Marvel Comics' ultimate universe as well. The Ultimate universe's Spider-Man saved Raimi and Tobey Maguire from the set of the movie after Doctor Octopus attacked it.

Reference: (http://marvel.wikia.com/wiki/Sam_Raimi_(Earth-1610))

468.

Douglas Adams, creator of the "Hitchhiker's Guide to the Galaxy" series, wanted Slartibartfast's name to sound very rude. He was originally called "Phartiphukborlz", and changed it gradually until the BBC accepted it for radio broadcast.

Reference: (https://en.wikipedia.org/wiki/Slartibartfast)

469.

Scientists use Wiffle Balls to measure coral. The spherical shape makes it omnidirectional and perfect for taking a speedy measurement, and the open design also allows it to avoid being crushed by water pressure.

Reference: (https://en.wikipedia.org/wiki/List_of_humorous_units_of_measurement)

470.

Riverside, California, now known as a rather impoverished place, was the wealthiest city per capita in the U.S. by 1895. This was fueled by the successful citrus industry, innovative irrigation systems, favorable climate and development of refrigerated rail cars.

Reference: (https://www.riversideca.gov/visiting-aboutriv.asp)

471.

Den Fujita, who opened the first McDonald's in Japan, believed if the Japanese ate McDonald's hamburgers and potatoes for one thousand years it would make the people taller, have white skin and turn their hair blonde.

Reference: (http://www.nytimes.com/2008/03/26/dining/26japan.html?pagewanted=1)

472.

The Beatles stopped touring in part because the audiences screamed so loud no one could hear them play.

Reference: (https://en.wikipedia.org/wiki/The_Beatles#Events_leading_up_to_final_tour)

473.

The Pentagon has twice as many toilet facilities needed for a building of its size because it had to conform to the Commonwealth of Virginia's racial segregation laws during construction.

Reference: (https://en.wikipedia.org/wiki/The_Pentagon#Construction)

474.

In 2012, an albatross named "Wisdom" hatched a new chick at the age of 62 and may have been the oldest mother in the bird world.

Reference: (https://blog.nationalgeographic.org/2014/02/04/6-of-the-worlds-longest-lived-animals/)

475.

A patent was awarded for a device that used centrifugal force to assist in childbirth.

Reference: (https://www.theatlantic.com/technology/archive/2011/10/old-very-weird-tech-an-apparatus-for-centrifugal-birthing/246186/)

476.

A Brazilian man once held a woman hostage for 10 hours with a Sega Light Phaser.

Reference: (https://kotaku.com/5160608/brazilian-man-holds-woman-hostage-for-10-hours-with-a-sega-light-gun)

477.

A fan of George R.R. Martin's "A Song of Ice and Fire" guessed that "Hodor" meant, "Hold the Door", to which Martin answered, "you don't know how close to the truth you are."

Reference: (https://www.telegraph.co.uk/tv/2016/05/23/how-george-rr-martin-had-game-of-thrones-hold-the-door-moment-pl/)

478.

During the Kelo Case, homeowners were evicted by the City of New London to build a private corporate development, only for the corporation to leave the city after the homes were demolished.

Reference:(https://en.wikipedia.org/wiki/Kelo_v._City_of_New_London#Subsequent_developments)

479.

Nevada City, in Nevada County, is located in California and not in the state of Nevada.

Reference: (https://en.wikipedia.org/wiki/Nevada_City,_California)

480.

"Roar" is the most dangerous movie ever made. The movie had 110 untrained lions, tigers, cheetahs, cougars and jaguars, which led to 70 cast and crew members being injured. The injuries ranged from broken bones to scalping and gangrene.

Reference: (https://www.theguardian.com/film/2015/apr/14/roar-review-big-cat-movie-that-injured-70-crew-is-re-released-run-towards-it)

481.

Shirley Temple, the iconic child star, served as ambassador to Czechoslovakia.

Reference: (https://en.wikipedia.org/wiki/Shirley_Temple)

482.

The Netherlands is known today as a haven for pedestrians and cyclists, however, in the 1970s, a growing epidemic of traffic deaths led to a national movement called "Stop the Child Murder." The results transformed the public spaces and street into some of the safest in the world.

Reference: (http://www.bbc.com/news/magazine-23587916)

483.

Over 90% of the 81,000 people adopted in Japan in 2011 were adult males in their 20s and 30s.

Reference: (https://en.wikipedia.org/wiki/Japanese_adult_adoption)

484.

The heaviest and oldest living organism is a tree named Pando, a Clonal Colony which roots are 80,000 years old, has 40,000 stems and weighs 6,000 metric tons.

Reference: (https://en.wikipedia.org/wiki/Pando_(tree))

485.

Congressman Clement Vallandigham, during the Civil War, gave a speech in Congress calling for peace negotiations. In response, Abraham Lincoln had him arrested for treason and turned over to the Confederates.

Reference: (https://en.wikipedia.org/wiki/Clement_Vallandigham)

486.

Flea, bassist for the Red Hot Chili Peppers, keeps over 200,000 bees in his backyard, which he calls "Flea's Bees".

Reference: (https://www.rollingstone.com/music/news/fleas-bees-chili-peppers-bassist-starts-apiary-20150816#)

487.

The small, cylindrical bumps on LEGO bricks are called "studs", and they are sometimes used as a measurement for the bricks.

Reference: (http://lego.wikia.com/wiki/Stud)

488.

Vin Diesel has played Dungeons and Dragons for 20 years, and even had a fake tattoo of his character's name on his stomach while filming "xXx".

Reference: (https://en.wikipedia.org/wiki/Vin_Diesel#Personal_life)

489.

The ship HNLMS Abraham Crijnssen was ordered to return to Australia after a Japanese attack. To avoid another ambush, the crew camouflaged the ship with jungle foliage to give the impression of a small island and traveled only at night. It was the only ship of its class to successfully arrive.

Reference: (https://en.wikipedia.org/wiki/HNLMS_Abraham_Crijnssen_(1936))

490.

After Michael Jordan dunked over 6'1'' guard John Stockton, an angry fan yelled at him to, "Pick on someone your own size". The next play he dunked over 6'11'' Mel Turpin. As he ran back down the floor, Jordan turned to the heckler and said, "Was he big enough?"

Reference: (https://sports.yahoo.com/blogs/ball-dont-lie/dunk-history--michael-jordan--and--was-he-big-enough--185521186.html)

491.

William Henry Perkin made his first discovery in the field of organic dye at the age of 18.

Reference: (https://en.wikipedia.org/wiki/William_Henry_Perkin)

492.

The word "gymnasium" comes from the Greek "gymons (γυμνός)", which means "naked" since in Ancient Greece, athletes exercised naked.

Reference: (https://attireclub.org/2015/05/31/culture-history-and-money-fashion-facts/)

493.

In 1982, a famous bootlegger, known simply as "Richard", compiled an entire album of various outtakes and blips from the late Elvis Presley's musical career, titled: "Elvis' Greatest Shit".

Reference: (https://en.wikipedia.org/wiki/Elvis%27_Greatest_Shit)

494.

There are 18 different forms of ice, which have completely different structures from one another, and occur at very different temperatures and pressures than "regular" ice.

Reference: (https://en.wikipedia.org/wiki/Ice#Phases)

495.

Serbia and Montenegro were represented by a single team in 2006 FIFA World Cup, despite having officially separated weeks before its start.

Reference: (https://en.wikipedia.org/wiki/Serbia_and_Montenegro)

496.

Charlie the macaw parrot, is 119 years old and allegedly belonged to Winston Churchill. The parrot can be heard yelling anti-Nazi slurs and cursing.

Reference: (http://scienceblogs.com/retrospectacle/2006/09/01/friday-grey-matters-the-myth-o/)

497.

"Hurricane Saturday," is a two-hour crossover 1991 television event between "The Golden Girls," its spinoff "Empty Nest," and Empty Nest's spinoff "Nurses." In other words, a back-to-back-to-back spinoff-to-spinoff.

Reference: (https://en.wikipedia.org/wiki/Hurricane_Saturday)

498.

In Russian, the use of some animal names as insults comes from prison slang. A goat is someone who informs the prison administration, and is a deadly insult. You can still get punched for calling a man a goat.

Reference: (https://www.rbth.com/lifestyle/327020-russians-animal-names)

499.

A survivor of the bombing of Hiroshima, Rev Tanimoto, was on an American television show in 1955 to raise money for the victims and was forced to meet and listen to the co-pilot of the Enola Gay talk about what he did.

Reference: (https://www.youtube.com/watch?v=l0m8D6APp64&feature=youtu.be)

500.

Dunking was banned in basketball from 1967 to 1976. The ban was known as the "Lew Alcindor Rule" which was Kareem Abdul-Jabbar's birth name.

Reference: (https://studioatgizmodo.kinja.com/a-look-back-at-the-ncaa-dunk-ban-and-forward-to-basketb-1505786580)

501.

The mangrove killifish is a fish that can spend up to 66 consecutive days living out of water.

Reference: (https://en.wikipedia.org/wiki/Mangrove_rivulus)

502.

Miles Browning, one of the most controversial and loathed U.S. Navy officers during World War II, is the grandfather of comedic actor Chevy Chase.

Reference: (https://www.usni.org/magazines/navalhistory/2016-04/out-jaws-victory)

503.

Carrie Underwood was only three credits away from earning her degree in Communications from Northeastern State University when she withdrew to participate in Season 4 of American Idol. She returned in 2006 and graduated magna cum laude after NSU decided to award her the remaining 3 credits.

Reference: (http://theboot.com/carrie-underwood-college/)

504.

The most successful pirate in history was a Chinese woman named Ching Shih. She commanded the Red Flag Fleet which consisted of 300 ships and 40,000 pirates. She was also one of the only pirates to actually retire.

Reference: (https://en.wikipedia.org/wiki/Ching_Shih)

505.

Everett Ruess, vagabond, writer and artist, wandered the wilderness of the High Sierra, the Californian coast and the American Southwest until his disappearance in a remote area of Utah. His fate remains a mystery to this day.

Reference: (https://en.wikipedia.org/wiki/Everett_Ruess)

506.

The rules about when to use "less" and "fewer" come from a preference Roger Baker had in 1770.

Reference: (https://www.copyoctopus.com/fewer-vs-less-grammatical-rule-needs-die/)

507.

Urban-dwelling birds sing at higher pitches to be heard over the noises of the city.

Reference: (https://undark.org/article/urban-ants-evolution-climate-change/)

508.

There is a term for when common words seem very strange, and it's called wordnesia.

Reference: (https://www.smithsonianmag.com/smart-news/when-even-simplest-word-looks-weird-and-wrong-you-have-wordnesia-180954539/)

509.

Many countries have official names that differ from what they are colloquially known. Among them are the official name for Greece: "Hellenic Republic", and the official name for Brunei: "Nation of Brunei, Abode of Peace".

Reference: (https://en.wikipedia.org/wiki/List_of_alternative_country_names)

510.

Tiger Woods spent 683 weeks as number 1 ranked golfer in the world. He spent 352 weeks more than any other player in OWGR history. Tiger's 79 tour wins are 67 more than any other player currently 40 or younger.

Reference: (http://www.golfchannel.com/article/golf-central-blog/stats-incredible-tigers-40-greatest-numerical-records/)

511.

Arthur Hailey's first script, "Flight Into Danger" was produced for the CBC by Sydney Newman, who later created "The Avengers" and "Doctor Who" and starred James Doohan, who played Scotty in "Star Trek".

Reference: (https://en.wikipedia.org/wiki/Flight_into_Danger)

512.

There is a hypothetical undiscovered planet in our solar system that is 10 times bigger than Earth.

Reference: (https://www.space.com/38431-new-evidence-planet-nine-existence.html)

513.

The Isle of Man is ranked by the World Bank as the 5th richest nation in the world by GDP per capita, with the largest sectors being insurance and eGaming with 17% of gross national product each.

Reference: (https://en.wikipedia.org/wiki/Economy_of_the_Isle_of_Man#eGaming_&_ICT)

514.

Pepperoni is a variety of salami created in the USA. The word was first used to describe the sausage in 1919.

Reference: (https://en.wikipedia.org/wiki/Pepperoni)

515.

Minnesota was the first state to ban added mercury, such as thimerosal, in cosmetics.

Reference: (https://www.cbsnews.com/news/minnesota-bans-adding-mercury-to-cosmetics/)

516.

James Cameron wanted to direct "Terminator" so badly, that he sold the rights to the producer willing to entertain his wish for $1. While waiting for Arnold Schwarzenegger to become available for the role, Cameron also busied himself by writing "Aliens" and "Rambo: First Blood Part II."

Reference: (http://www.achievement.org/achiever/james-cameron/)

517.

The "The NeverEnding Story" movie, despite having German producers, a German director and German screenplay authors and being based on a German book, shot mostly in Germany and released in Germany before the U.S., still was produced in English and features almost exclusively American actors.

Reference: (https://en.wikipedia.org/wiki/The_NeverEnding_Story_(film))

518.

The FDA, Food and Drug Administration, also regulates the use of lasers.

Reference: (https://www.fda.gov/Radiation-EmittingProducts/RadiationEmittingProductsandProcedures/HomeBusinessandEntertainment/LaserProductsandInstruments/default.htm)

519.

Atheist churches exist and they're styled after Mega Churches in the United States. Located in places like Dublin, Sydney, and New York, they are places for Atheists to replicate the Church experience.

Reference: (https://www.npr.org/2014/01/07/260184473/sunday-assembly-a-church-for-the-godless-picks-up-steam)

520.

As the HMS Sheffield was sinking off the Falklands in 1982, the crew gathered round and started singing "Always Look on the Bright Side of Life" from Monty Python.

Reference: (https://en.wikipedia.org/wiki/HMS_Sheffield_(D80)#Sinking)

521.

Until 1993, the BT Tower, a 200 meter tall building in the middle of London with a restaurant on top, did not "officially exist".

Reference: (https://en.wikipedia.org/wiki/BT_Tower#See_also)

522.

A deadly attack took place at the Turkish embassy in Ottawa, Ontario, Canada on March 12th, 1985; it was the 3rd attack against Turkish diplomatic staff, the other 2 happened during 1982.

Reference: (http://www.cbc.ca/archives/entry/1985-deadly-embassy-attack-in-ottawa)

523.

Theodore Geisel took up the pseudonym Dr. Seuss after being banned from his college humor magazine for drinking gin on campus during Prohibition.

Reference: (https://en.wikipedia.org/wiki/Dr._Seuss#Early_years)

524.

In the past 40 years, only one Best Picture winner has been released in the first four months of the year: The Silence of the Lambs, which was released on Valentine's Day.

Reference: (https://www.boxofficemojo.com/oscar/)

525.

The character Ari Gold from "Entourage" is based on real agent Ari Emanuel. He is alleged to have dismissed a Navy SEAL role for Wesley Snipes, saying, "Everyone knows that blacks don't swim".

Reference: (https://en.wikipedia.org/wiki/Ari_Emanuel)

526.

Hyperion, which is the tallest tree in the world, stands 380 feet tall and is over 800 years old.

Reference: (http://www.odditycentral.com/news/meet-hyperion-the-worlds-tallest-tree.html)

527.

There was a secret society known as "The Order of the Pug" where new members gained entrance by scratching at the door of the lodge and kissing the Grand Pug's backside under his tail as an expression of total devotion.

Reference: (https://nationalpurebreddogday.com/mopsorden-the-order-of-the-pug/)

528.

When Czechoslovakia split, the Czech Republic and Slovakia also split the national anthem, with each country getting one verse.

Reference: (https://en.wikipedia.org/wiki/Kde_domov_m%C5%AFj)

529.

There's a satellite in orbit that's running a Nexus 1 Android as one of its main CPU's.

Reference: (https://en.wikipedia.org/wiki/STRaND-1)

530.

James Earl Jones Was in the first production of New York City's "Shakespeare in the Park" in 1962.

Reference: (https://en.wikipedia.org/wiki/Delacorte_Theater)

531.

Honda revealed the shape of the B2 Bomber weeks before the government declassified it, in a car advertisement.

Reference: (https://jalopnik.com/how-honda-revealed-the-governments-top-secret-stealth-b-666462873)

532.

Comedian Demetri Martin incorporated music into his act to prevent Comedy Central from rearranging his performance for TV.

Reference: (https://www.youtube.com/watch?v=0fFTo3exnx8&feature=youtu.be&t=1h58m46s)

533.

After Emperor Nicephorus I burned and pillaged the Bulgarian capital Pliska he was ambushed and his 60,000 strong army wiped out by Bulgarian forces in 811. Khan Krum, who had defeated him, made a cup out of the Emperor's skull and drank wine from it.

Reference: (https://en.wikipedia.org/wiki/Battle_of_Pliska)

534.

The U.K. asked America to give back the original Winnie the Pooh bear. America said no.

Reference: (http://www.nytimes.com/1998/02/06/nyregion/pooh-cornered-blair-cedes-bear.html)

535.

Sasha Cohen and his crew had their lives threatened and could have been killed on more than one occasion while filming "Brüno."

Reference: (https://www.cinemablend.com/new/Incredible-War-Stories-From-Making-Bruno-13759.html)

536.

Marathon runners routinely lose their toenails due to bruising and friction. The constant rubbing and bruising on your toes can eventually cause the nails to dislodge and fall off. Doctors refer to it as "runner's toe" and it is a common annoyance for marathon runners.

Reference: (https://www.nbcnews.com/health/when-marathon-runners-leave-toenail-behind-1C6436947)

537.

Some people have a fourth cone in their eyes, allowing them to see an estimated 100 million extra nuances of color.

Reference: (https://www.popsci.com/article/science/woman-sees-100-times-more-colors-average-person#page-3)

538.

The largest ant supercolony in the world was estimated to have had billions of Argentine ants with millions of nests over a 6,000 kilometer area in southern Europe.

Reference: (https://en.wikipedia.org/wiki/Ant_colony#Colony_size)

539.

Texas celebrates their own Independence Day. The holiday commemorates the Texas Declaration of Independence which established the Republic of Texas, a decade long independence, before it officially joined the Union.

Reference: (https://en.wikipedia.org/wiki/Texas_Independence_Day#cite_note-1)

540.

Cheating on your spouse is a crime in New York, carrying a possible sentence of up to 6 months in jail.

Reference: (https://www.dbnylaw.com/adultery-is-still-a-crime-in-new-york-state/)

541.

All Mason Bees are solitary, meaning each female is a queen who does all of the chores. She can't gather pollen, lay eggs, gather mud, and defend her hole, so she doesn't. They're extremely gentle and allow you to confidently get inches from her nesting hole without fear of being stung.

Reference: (https://thehoneybeeconservancy.org/mason-bees/)

542.

British spree killer Joanna Dennehy called a friend after her third murder and sang the Britney Spears song, "Oops I Did it Again".

Reference: (http://www.bbc.com/news/uk-england-25669206)

543.

English is the most commonly spoken language in the world.

Reference: (https://www.weforum.org/agenda/2015/10/which-languages-are-most-widely-spoken/)

544.

In 1939, a trend swept across American colleges that involved swallowing live goldfish for a dare or publicity. One guy swallowed 67 goldfish in 14 minutes, while another set the record at 89 live goldfish in one sitting.

Reference: (http://www.mortaljourney.com/2011/01/1940-trends/goldfish-swallowing)

545.

John Joe Gray was involved in the longest law enforcement standoff in U.S. history. It lasted just under 15 years before the charges were dropped.

Reference: (https://en.wikipedia.org/wiki/John_Joe_Gray)

546.

The first personal lift was built for King Louis XV to move discreetly between the first and second floor of his apartment to visit his mistress.

Reference: (http://olympiclifts.co.uk/historical-lifts-made-first-lift/)

547.

There are about 187,888 lakes in Finland.

Reference: (https://en.wikipedia.org/wiki/List_of_lakes_of_Finland)

548.

The famous London Underground subway system has a companion above-ground service, the London Overground.

Reference: (https://en.wikipedia.org/wiki/London_Overground)

549.

Bangladesh has the fastest GDP growth rate of any country. Nearly double that of China.

Reference: (https://en.wikipedia.org/wiki/List_of_countries_by_real_GDP_growth_rate)

550.

In the New York Harbor, among many other strange finds, The Army Corps of Engineers once located a grand piano and a giraffe carcass.

Reference: (http://nymag.com/news/features/56609/)

551.

There's a borough in Pennsylvania called East Berlin, and it was called that over 150 years before the Berlin Wall.

Reference: (https://en.wikipedia.org/wiki/East_Berlin,_Pennsylvania?q=East+Berlin%2C+Pennsylvania&_ext=EiQp+wEwGgn4Q0AxUMso+cU+U8A5+wEwGgn4Q0BBUMso+cU+U8A%3D)

552.

The reason infants can't eat honey is because it contains botulism spores which their digestive systems aren't developed enough to prevent from developing.

Reference: (https://www.poison.org/articles/2010-jun/dont-feed-honey-to-infants)

553.

In 1857, engineers constructing the Lahor-Multan railroad used the bricks from the Harappan Ruins for track ballasts.

Reference: (https://en.wikipedia.org/wiki/Harappa#History)

554.

The 1972 pornographic film, "Deep Throat," reportedly earned as much as $600 million, which, if true, would make it a higher grossing film than Star Wars, though this figure may have been inflated by gangsters who used movie theaters in money laundering schemes.

Reference: (https://en.wikipedia.org/w/index.php?title=List_of_highest-grossing_films&mobileaction=toggle_view_desktop#Timeline_of_highest-grossing_films)

555.

The country of Liechtenstein did not recognize Czechia over disputed land within Czechia that was ten times the size of Liechtenstein.

Reference: (http://www.radio.cz/en/section/curraffrs/czech-republic-to-restore-diplomatic-relations-with-liechtenstein)

556.

Short intense exercise improves cardio-metabolic health equally to traditional endurance training, but short intense exercise takes only one fifth the time spent exercising.

Reference: (http://journals.plos.org/plosone/article?id=10.1371/journal.pone.0154075)

557.

People really do judge books by their covers. A massive 79% of people admit that a book cover plays a decisive role in whether or not they purchase a book. Moreover, 40% of people will change their minds about buying a book they already wanted, if it has a bad cover.

Reference: (https://www.thebooksmugglers.com/2010/04/cover-matters-the-survey-results.html)

558.

Benjamin Franklin was not behind the idea of daylight savings time. In 1784, he sent a satirical essay to a French newspaper, it has been credited to him ever since.

Reference: (https://www.thedenverchannel.com/news/trending/benjamin-franklin-world-war-1-and-daylight-saving-time)

559.

R. Kelly was 27 when he illegally married singer Aaliyah, who was 15 years old, who falsely stated her age as 18.

Reference: (https://en.wikipedia.org/wiki/Aaliyah)

560.

The difference between a pond and a lake is depth.

Reference: (https://www.lakemat.com/whats-the-difference-between-a-lake-and-a-pond/)

561.

Most Germans sing "Happy Birthday" in English but with a German accent, rather than singing it in German

Reference: (http://angelikasgerman.co.uk/how-do-the-germans-sing-happy-birthday/)

562.

Glima is a Scandinavian martial art similar to modern wrestling that was used by the Vikings.

Reference: (https://en.wikipedia.org/wiki/Glima)

563.

Many people harbor remnants of Neanderthal DNA, which is theorized to offer significant health benefits, including boosting the immune system.

Reference: (https://www.the-scientist.com/?articles.view/articleNo/47474/title/Advantages-of-Neanderthal-DNA-in-the-Human-Genome/)

564.

Your right ear is better than your left ear at receiving sounds from speech, whereas your left ear is more sensitive to sounds of music and song.

Reference: (https://www.hear-it.org/Your-ears-differ-)

565.

Barbara Stanwyck, one of the most famous Hollywood actresses of all time, never won an Academy Award, except for an honorary in 1982.

Reference: (https://en.wikipedia.org/wiki/Barbara_Stanwyck#Awards_and_nominations)

566.

The Szondi Test is a test designated to explain your subconscious drive through varying photos of 18th to 19th century mental asylum patients and choosing the one that scares you the most.

Reference: (https://en.wikipedia.org/wiki/Szondi_test)

567.

During its prime, Atari created their "competitor", Kee Games, to help distribute more game cartridges.

Reference: (https://www.giantbomb.com/kee-games/3010-8456/)

568.

Gedhun Choekyi Nyima, the 11th Panchen Lama, the person responsible for choosing the next Dalai Lama, was kidnapped and replaced in 1995 by the Chinese Government when he was only 6 years old. No one has heard from him or his family since.

Reference: (https://www.huffingtonpost.com/us/entry/7308598)

569.

Robert Opel streaked the 1974 Oscars, then ran for president with the slogan "Not Just Another Crooked Dick" in 1976, and then was suspiciously murdered at his gay art studio in 1979.

Reference: (https://en.wikipedia.org/wiki/Robert_Opel#Life)

570.

The Anti-Masonic Party, in the 1832 Presidential Election, nominated a former Freemason who publicly defended the Freemasons during his campaign.

Reference: (https://en.wikipedia.org/wiki/William_Wirt_(Attorney_General)#Later_life_and_Presidential_run)

571.

The astrophysicist term "black hole" is named after the "Black Hole of Calcutta" because physicist Robert Dicke in the early 1960s compared such gravitationally collapsed objects to the infamous prison.

Reference: (https://en.wikipedia.org/wiki/Black_Hole_of_Calcutta#Astronomy)

572.

When the President of the United States travels outside of North America in Air Force One, an E-4B plane, or "Nightwatch", deploys to an airport in the vicinity of the President's destination. It is a mobile command post for the National Command Authority to be available in the event of a world crisis.

Reference: (https://en.wikipedia.org/wiki/Boeing_E-4)

573.

Each commercial airplane in the U.S. is struck by lightning more than once every year on average.

Reference: (https://www.scientificamerican.com/article/what-happens-when-lightni/)

574.

Jerome Jacobson was the only real winner of the McDonalds Monopoly from 1995 to 2000.

Reference: (https://www.thebalance.com/mcdonald s-monopoly-game-scam-or-legitimate-sweepstakes-896846)

575.

The first international soccer match was played between Scotland and England in 1872. Scotland played with 6 forwards, England played with 8. The match finished 0-0.

Reference: (https://www.theguardian.com/football/2016/nov/11/england-scotland-first-football-fixture-1872)

576.

Late last year, archeologists in Israel discovered a cave that was used by humans some 400,000 years ago. They think it was used as a "school" where people were taught how to make primitive tools.

Reference: (https://www.fromthegrapevine.com/lifestyle/newly-discovered-400000-year-old-school-israel-qesem-cave)

577.

The hooded pitohui of New Guinea is a song bird whose skin contains a neurotoxin powerful enough to numb the hands if not handled with gloves. Some scientists believe the birds may rub the toxin on their eggs to protect them, but its true purpose is still up for debate.

Reference: (https://en.wikipedia.org/wiki/Hooded_pitohui#Ecology)

578.

Even anticipating exercise elevates your breathing and heart rate, increasing blood flow, dilating blood vessels and jumpstarting energy pathways.

Reference: (https://healthyliving.azcentral.com/breathing-rates-increase-before-exercise-18758.html)

579.

The Honeyguide is an African bird that evolved alongside early humans and leads humans to honey.

Reference: (https://en.wikipedia.org/wiki/Greater_honeyguide)

580.

Two brewers, Evil Twin and Lervig Aktiebryggeri, made a beer using actual frozen pizzas and money.

Reference: (http://www.grubstreet.com/2015/10/frozen-pizza-money-beer.html)

581.

If you have at least one grandparent that was born in Ireland then you're eligible for Irish citizenship.

Reference:(http://www.citizensinformation.ie/en/moving_country/irish_citizenship/irish_citizenship_through_birth_or_descent.html#l091af)

582.

Rose Royce's "Wishing on a Star" was played every Saturday at noon on Kiss 108 Boston for 26 years until 2004.

Reference: (https://en.wikipedia.org/wiki/Wishing_on_a_Star)

583.

Keegan-Michael Key is the half-brother of Dwayne McDuffie, creator of "Static Shock" and "Ben 10".

Reference: (https://en.wikipedia.org/wiki/Keegan-Michael_Key#Early_life)

584.

Khassan Baiev was the only surgeon for over 80,000 people during the Chechen wars and, at one point, during the conflict he performed 67 amputations and eight brain operations in a 48-hour period. He was also known for treating both Chechen and Russian soldiers.

Reference: (https://en.wikipedia.org/wiki/Khassan_Baiev)

585.

The Yiddish expression "Nu?" is far more than an interjection meaning, "Go on." Depending on tone and context, this one word scan speak volumes.

Reference: (https://forward.com/culture/12736/just-say-nu-01335/)

586.

The Dalmatian dog breed traces its roots to the region of Dalmatia, Croatia.

Reference: (https://en.wikipedia.org/wiki/Dalmatian_dog)

587.

Antifreeze from fish blood keeps low-fat ice cream rich and creamy.

Reference: (https://www.nextnature.net/2012/09/antifreeze-protein-from-fish-blood-keeps-low-fat-ice-cream-rich-and-creamy/)

588.

"Plogging" is a growing sport that combines jogging with picking up litter.

Reference: (https://en.wikipedia.org/wiki/Plogging)

589.

The inspiration of the German ship in "The African Queen" still plies the waters of Lake Tanganyika. Built in 1913, the ship was first assembled and then dismantled into hundreds of individual parts to be packed and shipped to Africa. The journey continued overland across Africa to the lake.

Reference:(http://www.meyerwerft.de/en/meyerwerft_de/werft/unternehmensgeschichte/graf_goetzen/graf_goetzen.jsp)

590.

The I-5 killer, Randall Woodfield, had a college football career and was even drafted by the Green Bay Packers.

Reference:(https://en.wikipedia.org/wiki/Randall_Woodfield#College_years_and_football_career)

591.

Camp Siegfried, a summer camp which taught Nazi ideology, existed in New York in the 1930s.

Reference: (https://en.wikipedia.org/wiki/Camp_Siegfried)

592.

The Democratic Party of China, or DPC, convened its first Congress on August 13th, 2006, in the Sheraton Hotel of Flushing, Queens, New York. A total of 111 delegates from all the provinces, municipalities and autonomous regions of China attended the Congress.

Reference: (https://en.wikipedia.org/wiki/Democracy_Party_of_China)

593.

Mao Zedong was originally an anarchist when he became a librarian's assistant at Peking University.

Reference: (https://en.wikipedia.org/wiki/Early_revolutionary_activity_of_Mao_Zedong)

594.

The Edenton Tea Party was a boycott inspired by the Boston Tea Party, which was organized entirely by women in Edenton, North Carolina.

Reference: (https://en.wikipedia.org/wiki/Edenton_Tea_Party)

595.

Boney M was founded by singer-composer Frank Farian because he was too embarrassed to perform "Baby Do You Wanna Bump" himself, a song he'd recorded doing all the voices, including the female ones.

Reference: (https://www.youtube.com/watch?v=K1bbacT7BsY)

596.

There was a captive toad that reached the age of 40.

Reference:(http://www.yorkpress.co.uk/news/9038208.Meet_Georgie___the__world_s_oldest_toad/)

597.

In 1941, a zoo keeper, George Lewis, once fought an elephant that attacked him with his bare hands, escaping after stunning the animal by punching it in the eye.

Reference: (https://en.wikipedia.org/wiki/Ziggy_(elephant)#Attack_on_Slim_Lewis)

598.

Greyfriars Bobby is the dog who sat by his owner's grave 14 years after his passing, somewhat inspiring the "Futurama" episode Jurassic Bark.

Reference: (http://www.historic-uk.com/HistoryUK/HistoryofScotland/Greyfriars-Bobby/)

599.

Corinthian leather was a made up word for a Chrysler commercial.

Reference: (https://www.youtube.com/watch?v=3p9g3JCZv1E&feature=youtu.be)

600.

There is a rock cover band called the Wackids that exclusively uses mini and children's instruments.

Reference: (https://youtu.be/Xqz5WGNfiSw)

601.

The word "lunatic" was derived from "lunaticus", which directly translates to "moon-struck", since it was once thought that some mental illnesses were caused by a full moon.

Reference: (https://www.scientificamerican.com/article/lunacy-and-the-full-moon/)

602.

Sharon Lopatka met a man online and asked to be tortured to death. It was reportedly the first case where a police department arrested a murder suspect with evidence primarily gathered from email messages.

Reference: (https://www.independent.co.uk/life-style/on-22-august-sharon-lopatka-set-out-to-look-for-someone-to-kill-her-so-she-posted-an-internet-1351937.html)

603.

The city of Amman, Jordan was named "Philadelphia" during ancient Greek rule.

Reference: (https://en.wikipedia.org/wiki/Amman#Classical_period)

604.

While 58.9% of Americans over 25 have "some college" education, only 32.5% have a bachelor's degree or higher. Also, native born Americans and foreign born Americans have almost identical educational achievement rates.

Reference: (https://www.census.gov/content/dam/Census/library/publications/2016/demo/p20-578.pdf)

605.

The Amazon rainforest is not actually natural, but has instead been shaped by the native people for thousands of years.

Reference: (https://www.smithsonianmag.com/science-nature/pristine-untouched-amazonian-rainforest-was-actually-shaped-humans-180962378/)

606.

Tori Spelling and Randy Spelling, children of famous Hollywood producer Aaron Spelling, only received $800,000 each of their father's $600 million dollar fortune.

Reference: (https://www.reelz.com/extra/aaron-spelling-left-behind-massive-fortune-broken-family/)

607.

After British ex-Prime Minister Margaret Thatcher died, a campaign was started to bring "Ding Dong the Witch is Dead" from "The Wizard of Oz" to the top of the music charts. It sold over 50,000 copies and entered at Number Two.

Reference: (http://www.bbc.co.uk/news/entertainment-arts-22145306)

608.

In 2015, a Louisiana man was arrested for drunkenly riding a horse on a highway. When detained, he said, "The horse knows the way home", and the sheriff concluded it did not constitute DUI.

Reference: (http://www.insideedition.com/headlines/11942-man-accused-of-drunkenly-riding-his-horse-on-a-highway-says-the-horse-knows-the)

609.

The population of Ireland has never recovered from the potato famine.

Reference: (https://en.wikipedia.org/wiki/Irish_population_analysis)

610.

Julian Jaynes's "Bicameral Mind Theory" suggests that ancient humans were not self-aware and that the right hemisphere communicated with the left via auditory hallucinations. These voices may have been interpreted as "gods" by early humans.

Reference: (http://nautil.us/issue/24/error/consciousness-began-when-the-gods-stopped-speaking)

611.

U.S. citizens can get a valid, second passport.

Reference: (https://passportinfo.com/second-passport/)

612.

Maimonides stated that, "It is better and more satisfactory to acquit a thousand guilty persons than to put a single innocent one to death." Maimonides argued that executing a defendant on anything less than absolute certainty would lead to a slippery slope of decreasing burdens of proof.

Reference: (https://en.wikipedia.org/wiki/Capital_and_corporal_punishment_in_Judaism)

613.

Bob Widlar installed "The Hassler" outside his office. Whenever people started talking, the device would detect the audio, convert it to high frequency, and playback the converted sound. Visitors would notice this ringing, stop talking, and the sound disappeared.

Reference: (https://www.autodesk.com/products/eagle/blog/bob-widlar-life-engineering-legend/)

614.

Because of Daylight Savings Time and the loss of an hour of sleep, the Monday after clocks "Spring Forward" sees an increase in fatal traffic accidents.

Reference: (https://www.ncbi.nlm.nih.gov/m/pubmed/11152980/)

615.

Walruses are related to dogs and raccoons.

Reference: (https://en.wikipedia.org/wiki/Caniformia)

616.

The Orgone Accumulator was a device sold in the 1950s to allow a person sitting inside to attract orgone, a massless "healing energy". The FDA noted that one purchaser, a college professor, knew it was "phony" but found it, "helpful because his wife sat quietly in it for four hours every day."

Reference: (https://en.wikipedia.org/wiki/Wilhelm_Reich?repost#Injunction)

617.

In curling, good sportsmanship and politeness are essential. Congratulating opponents and abstaining from trash talk are part of what's known as the "Spirit of Curling."

Reference: (http://cornwallcurling.com/2014/12/04/curling-etiquette-basic-rules-code-of-ethics/)

618.

Part of the cause of the Great Depression was that both banks claimed to have the money when someone from bank A wrote a check to someone from bank B, wildly overstating how much money was in circulation.

Reference: (https://www.federalreservehistory.org/essays/banking_panics_1930_31)

619.

The technology behind color photography was based on white skin, called "normal". Technological bias still exists somewhat today.

Reference: (https://youtu.be/d16LNHIEJzs)

620.

There are more men named John running Fortune 100 companies than women altogether.

Reference: (https://amp.theguardian.com/business/2015/mar/06/johns-davids-and-ians-outnumber-female-chief-executives-in-ftse-100)

621.

There are countries whose first day of the week is Saturday.

Reference: (http://chartsbin.com/view/41671)

622.

Robert Altman, who directed the movie "M*A*S*H", despised the television series which followed his film, citing it as being the antithesis of what his movie was about.

Reference: (https://en.wikipedia.org/wiki/Robert_Altman#Personal_life)

623.

In her book "To Kill a Mocking Bird", Harper Lee had based the character of Scout's best friend, Charles Baker "Dill" Harris on her childhood best friend Truman Capote.

Reference: (https://mom.me/lifestyle/9673-real-people-behind-famous-childrens-characters/item/truman-capote-charles-baker-dill-harris-kill-mockingbird/)

624.

Powerful earthquakes can shorten the length of the day. The 8.9 earthquake that hit Japan in 2011 accelerated Earth's spin, reducing the length of the day by 1.8 microseconds.

Reference: (https://www.space.com/11115-japan-earthquake-shortened-earth-days.html)

625.

While recording "Appetite for Destruction", Slash used a mudded amp head that was a rental. After recording, he kept the amp head but the rental company eventually repoed it.

Reference: (https://www.youtube.com/watch?v=nEq1tKM4v2k&feature=youtu.be&t=1021)

626.

All arcade games imported into North America from 1989 to 2000 had the following FBI slogan included into their attract mode: "Winners Don't Use Drugs".

Reference: (https://en.wikipedia.org/wiki/Winners_Don%27t_Use_Drugs)

627.

Poet and author Maya Angelou became San Francisco's first black female streetcar conductor, at the age of 16.

Reference: (http://sfist.com/2014/05/28/how_maya_angelou_became_san_francis.php)

628.

The fastest unassisted cyclist rode 83 miles per hour on flat terrain. The fastest unassisted upright cyclist rode 51 miles per hour.

Reference: (https://en.wikipedia.org/wiki/List_of_cycling_records)

629.

Engrish is named Engrish because it is hard for Japanese people to distinguish between the letters "L" and "R."

Reference: (https://en.wikipedia.org/wiki/Engrish)

630.

Bela Lugosi was buried in one of his "Dracula" costumes at the request of his wife and son.

Reference: (https://en.wikipedia.org/wiki/Bela_Lugosi#Death)

631.

The difference between Shia and Sunni Muslims is who they believe is the rightful successor to Muhammad. Sunnis believe that the 4 Caliphs that came to power after his death where chosen by him. Shias believe that he chose as his successor his cousin and son-in-law Ali.

Reference: (https://en.wikipedia.org/wiki/Rashidun)

632.

The main piece of the math equation for stealth technology was discovered by accident when a scientist stumbled upon it reading a 20 year old academic paper.

Reference: (https://www.youtube.com/watch?v=yiIbeMdqM90&feature=youtu.be&t=36m12s)

633.

Albert Einstein's second wife, Elsa Einstein, was his first cousin.

Reference: (https://en.wikipedia.org/wiki/Elsa_Einstein)

634.

Eleanor Roosevelt was instrumental in the writing of the Universal Declaration of Human Rights.

Reference: (https://www.amnesty.org.uk/universal-declaration-human-rights-UDHR)

635.

NASA actually has an Office of Planetary Protection in case life is found on another planet.

Reference: (https://planetaryprotection.nasa.gov/about)

636.

The U.S. Postal Service's unofficial motto was first used in 440 BC by Herodotus, who was impressed by the Persian Empire's messenger system.

Reference: (https://en.wikipedia.org/wiki/Angarium)

637.

A Continental Airlines Flight 11 went down in 1962 to a suicide bombing on board by a married man to help his family claim $300,000 worth of insurance money. The policy was later voided and the widow was only able to claim a $3 refund.

Reference: (https://en.wikipedia.org/wiki/Continental_Airlines_Flight_11)

638.
Arizona and Hawaii don't observe Daylight Savings Time.

Reference: (https://www.azcentral.com/story/travel/2017/03/06/why-arizona-doesnt-observe-daylight-saving-time/98639074/)

639.
Brandon Cruz, who played Eddie on "The Courtship of Eddie's Father," is a punk singer who was lead vocalist for the Dead Kennedys.

Reference: (https://youtu.be/mIE9Ff5vzLk)

640.
A sculpture of Spider-Man on a shopping mall in South Korea was removed because the artist showed the super hero with an erection.

Reference: (https://www.huffingtonpost.com/2014/06/09/spider-man-erection_n_5473089.html)

641.
Sade's "Diamond Life" sold over six million copies, making her the best-selling debut by a British female vocalist. By the time she performed her first live show, she was so popular that 1,000 people were turned away at the door.

Reference: (https://en.wikipedia.org/wiki/Sade_(singer)#Musical_career)

642.
Contrary to the idea of it being a scam, multiple medical organizations have endorsed chiropractic management for lower back pain. Studies have shown that chiropractic treatment is just as effective as conventional options for lower back pain management.

Reference: (https://nccih.nih.gov/health/pain/spinemanipulation.htm)

643.
After Britney Spears was admitted to a psych ward 10 years ago, Associated Press started preparing an obituary.

Reference: (http://www.nydailynews.com/entertainment/ap-prepares-britney-spears-obit-article-1.343771)

644.

In Tokyo, there is a huge arcade made to look like a dystopian cyberpunk city.

Reference: (https://www.atlasobscura.com/places/anata-no-warehouse)

645.

Baby walkers are illegal in Canada. Even selling an old one at a yard sale is illegal.

Reference: (https://www.babycenter.ca/x554838/should-i-use-a-baby-walker)

646.

Only 16 of the 39 Mars missions have been successful.

Reference: (https://theplanets.org/mars/)

647.

Robert Hooke, despite pioneering the experimental method and discovering many elements of gravitational theory first, was almost entirely erased from history by Sir Isaac Newton because they did not like each other and Newton lived 25 years longer, allowing him to edit history in his favor.

Reference: (https://www.telegraph.co.uk/news/uknews/1422928/Pioneering-scientist-erased-by-Newton.html)

648.

Male ducks often force themselves into females and have corkscrew shaped penises so that they deposit their sperm further into the female than their rivals. To counter this, females develop vaginas that are equally long and twisted.

Reference: (http://phenomena.nationalgeographic.com/2009/12/22/ballistic-penises-and-corkscrew-vaginas-the-sexual-battles-of-ducks/?_ga=2.154332536.1941308955.1520765767-364378408.1520765765)

649.

During the Battle of Manners Street, in 1943, over a thousand men fought in the streets of Wellington, New Zealand after American soldiers refused Maori from entering the Allied Services Club. It was not the only clash between U.S. and N.Z. soldiers in New Zealand during the war.

Reference: (https://teara.govt.nz/en/1966/riots/page-7)

650.

Male peacock spiders use complex movement, vibrations, and color to win the females over, a new study confirms. But the females are not easily impressed by the males' disco dance.

Reference: (https://news.nationalgeographic.com/2015/12/151201-australia-peacock-spider-colorful-courtship-sex-animals-science/)

651.

Skarð, a village on the Feroes Islands, was abandoned in 1913, when the entire male population perished on a fishing accident.

Reference: (https://en.wikipedia.org/wiki/Skar%C3%B0)

652.

Princess Beatrice has dyslexia. She delayed doing her exams for a year as a result of the condition.

Reference: (https://en.wikipedia.org/wiki/Princess_Beatrice_of_York)

653.

There is between 7% and 14% of the world's population that dislike cilantro due to 8 olfactory receptor genes. One in particular OR6A2, is why some perceive a soapy taste.

Reference: (https://www.nature.com/news/soapy-taste-of-coriander-linked-to-genetic-variants-1.11398)

654.

Pommer's Law, one of the "Laws" of the Internet, states. "A person's mind can be changed by reading information on the internet. The nature of this change will be from having no opinion to having a wrong opinion."

Reference: (https://www.telegraph.co.uk/technology/news/6408927/Internet-rules-and-laws-the-top-10-from-Godwin-to-Poe.html)

655.

On the DVD release of "Borat," there is a language option for Hebrew, but choosing it only results in a warning screen reading, "You have been trapped, Jew!"

Reference: (https://wikipedia.org/wiki/Borat#Home_media)

656.

In 2006, German filmmaker Uwe Boll, widely regarded as one of the worst directors in the world, challenged five of his harshest critics to a 10-round boxing match. The fights went ahead, in an event dubbed "Raging Boll", and Boll went on to beat all his opponents.

Reference: (https://www.wired.com/2006/12/ragingboll/)

657.

The 2000 film "The Million Dollar Hotel" produced by Bono with a soundtrack by U2 was a major flop. Star Mel Gibson didn't help when, tired after a long day of interviews, said, "I thought it was as boring as a dog's ass".

Reference: (https://en.wikipedia.org/wiki/The_Million_Dollar_Hotel)

658.

Howard Dully received a lobotomy at the age of 12, causing him a life of hardship. He discovered what happened to him later in life, and wrote a New York Times bestselling memoir about his experience.

Reference: (https://en.wikipedia.org/wiki/Howard_Dully)

659.

The brand name Kate Spade is a combination of the names of its husband and wife founders. Andy Spade, the husband, is the brother of David Spade.

Reference: (https://en.wikipedia.org/wiki/Kate_Spade_New_York)

660.

Owen Wilson attempted suicide and was subsequently treated for depression. A few days after his hospitalization, Wilson withdrew from his role in "Tropic Thunder." He was replaced by Matthew McConaughey.

Reference: (https://en.wikipedia.org/wiki/Owen_Wilson#Filmography)

661.

Bambi Woods, who was best known for her appearance as the title character in the 1978 film "Debbie Does Dallas," has disappeared since 1986. Mostly because Jim Clark, who coined Woods's stage name, has refused to divulge her real name out of respect for her requests for privacy.

Reference: (https://en.wikipedia.org/wiki/Bambi_Woods)

662.

Chip is short for Charles.

Reference: (https://www.behindthename.com/name/chip)

663.

The 2002 game "Darkened Skye," despite no mention on the box cover or cross promotion, featured heavy product placement of Skittles candy which all magic use was based around.

Reference: (https://en.wikipedia.org/wiki/Darkened_Skye)

664.

Byford Dolphin is an oil rig which has suffered some serious accidents, most notably an explosive decompression leading to a member of the crew being sucked through a 24 inch diameter hole.

Reference: (https://en.wikipedia.org/wiki/Byford_Dolphin)

665.

The U.S. Government acknowledged that the takeover of Hawaii by a group of American missionary descendants was illegal and unethical yet never intervened, leading to the annexation of Hawaii. Also, this group's first president was Sanford Dole, cousin of the founder of what is today the Dole Food Company.

Reference: (https://youtu.be/m3jnu0zhZrU?t=4391)

666.

After the War of 1812, America went through the "Era of Good Feelings". During this period, America experienced national unity and had only one political party, the Democratic-Republicans.

Reference: (https://en.wikipedia.org/wiki/Era_of_Good_Feelings)

667.

The King Cobra is not a cobra and makes a barking sound.

Reference: (https://www.nationalgeographic.com/animals/reptiles/k/king-cobra/)

668.

In the 1908 London Olympics, the Russian team arrived 12 days late and missed their most favored event because they were still following the Julian calendar rather than the Gregorian calendar.

Reference: (https://www.sports-reference.com/olympics/summer/1908/SHO/mens-military-rifle-200-500-600-800-900-1000-yards-team.html)

669.

The Walk of Life Project replaces the songs at the ends of movies with Dire Straits "Walk of Life" because, "it makes every movie 400% better".

Reference: (http://www.wolproject.com/)

670.

The Village People were banned in the Soviet Union because they were "violent."

Reference:(http://www.nzherald.co.nz/entertainment/news/article.cfm?c_id=1501119&objectid=11270086)

671.

Glenn Danzig, founder of the Misfits, was offered the role of Wolverine in the first X-men movie.

Reference: (https://en.wikipedia.org/wiki/Glenn_Danzig#cite_note-knight-ridder-73)

672.

One of Clarke's Three Laws state, "The only way of discovering the limits of the possible is to venture a little way past them into the impossible."

Reference: (https://en.wikipedia.org/wiki/Clarke%27s_three_laws)

673.

Beethoven wrote arrangements for over 150 English language folksongs.

Reference: (http://www.triovanbeethoven.at/cms_site_en/Programmes/Folksong-Arrangements-by-Haydn-and-Beethoven/Folksong-Arrangements-by-Beethoven)

674.

The 100 man kumite is a challenge of 100 sparring matches lasting 2 minutes each. Created in the 1950s, it was first completed by its creator, 3 times in 3 consecutive days. The next person to complete was in 1965.

Reference: (http://www.blackbeltwiki.com/100-man-kumite)

675.

Eating too many pine nuts at once can give you "pine mouth", where everything you eat has a bitter or metallic taste, even candy. The condition can last up to 2 weeks.

Reference: (http://www.foodauthority.nsw.gov.au/aboutus/science/food-risk-studies/pine-nuts-and-pine-mouth)

676.

Traffic jams can appear for no apparent reason.

Reference: (https://www.youtube.com/watch?v=Suugn-p5C1M)

677.

Kiefer Sutherland's full name is Kiefer William Frederick Dempsey George Rufus Sutherland.

Reference: (https://en.wikipedia.org/wiki/Kiefer_Sutherland)

678.

Arizona sponsors a beer brewing challenge for brewers willing to use "purified" raw sewage.

Reference: (http://www.azpurewaterbrew.org/faqs.html)

679.

In Australia, it is against the law to crush a can of beer between your breasts.

Reference: (http://www.news.com.au/news/can-crushing-barmaid-in-hiding/news-story/a2ed8fa52c757d272ccf752097ba0a0c)

680.

In the USA, it's considered the norm for cats to be kept inside. In the U.K., it's the complete opposite.

Reference: (http://messybeast.com/indooroutdoor.htm)

681.

Hulk Hogan's final WCW contract had clauses paying him $20,000 per month to wear New World Order T-Shirts and allowed him to license his image for, "Pasta, pasta restaurants, sandwiches, sun tan oil, health drink mixers and vitamins."

Reference: (https://www.scribd.com/doc/287131780/1998-Hulk-Hogan-contract-with-WCW)

682.

In 1959, Entenmann's created the see-through cake box.

Reference: (https://en.wikipedia.org/wiki/Entenmann%27s#History)

683.

The struggle session was a form of public humiliation and torture used by the Communist Party of China. The victim of a struggle session was forced to admit to various crimes before a crowd of people who would verbally and physically abuse the victim until he or she confessed.

Reference: (https://en.wikipedia.org/wiki/Struggle_session)

684.

The final battle scene in "The Last Jedi" was filmed on Salar de Uyuni, the world's largest salt flat in Bolivia. By some estimates, more than 10 billion tons of salt cover the region today and it is home to more than 50 percent of the world's lithium reserves.

Reference: (https://www.mnn.com/earth-matters/wilderness-resources/blogs/last-jedi-battle-filmed-earths-largest-salt-flat-salar-de-uyuni)

685.

Warren Buffet and Quicken Loans offered to pay someone $1 billion if they got their March Madness bracket 100% correct.

Reference: (https://www.usatoday.com/story/money/personalfinance/2014/03/17/ncaa-march-madness-bracket-1-billion-prize/6524153/)

686.

Nazi Germany made medals commemorating the acquisition of various territories.

Reference: (https://en.wikipedia.org/wiki/German_Occupation_Medals)

687.

There's a Darth Vader sculpture on the National Cathedral in Washington, D.C.

Reference: (https://www.atlasobscura.com/places/darth-vader-grotesque)

688.

In 2013, a zoo in China tried to pass off a hairy dog as a lion.

Reference: (https://edition.cnn.com/2013/08/16/world/asia/china-zoo-dog-lion/index.html)

689.

Apple and Facebook's medical benefits include egg-freezing for their female employees.

Reference: (https://www.npr.org/sections/alltechconsidered/2014/10/17/356765423/silicon-valley-companies-add-new-benefit-for-women-egg-freezing)

690.

The show "Portlandia" was banned from a feminist bookstore in Portland for their skits. They claimed that Fred Armisen's dressing as a woman was derogatory mockery towards trans women. They're no longer welcome to film in the location.

Reference: (https://www.npr.org/sections/thetwo-way/2016/09/30/496072761/feminist-bookstore-slams-portlandia-and-says-show-can-no-longer-film-there)

691.

There is a bridge constructed for use only by crabs.

Reference:(https://www.telegraph.co.uk/news/worldnews/australiaandthepacific/australia/12045930/Crabs-get-their-own-bridge-to-cross-busy-road-on-Christmas-Island.html)

692.

The oscillated icefish doesn't have any hemoglobin in its blood, which makes it clear.

Reference: (https://www.popsci.com/science/article/2013-04/weird-fish-has-clear-blood)

693.

The U.S. Department of Transportation owns and operates a nuclear powered cargo vessel.

Reference: (https://www.marad.dot.gov/ships-and-shipping/n-s-savannah-program-home/)

694.

The Ottomans' elite soldiers, called janissaries, were made of kidnapped European boys who trained in Spartan conditions under eunuchs. They eventually threatened the Sultan's power, so he killed over 4,000 of them in a carefully planned plot.

Reference: (https://en.wikipedia.org/wiki/Janissaries)

695.

Chuck Norris is 78 years old and once trained with Bruce Lee, fighting him in the film "Way of the Dragon." He is also a fan of "Chuck Norris Facts," appearing on many shows sharing his favorites.

Reference: (https://en.wikipedia.org/wiki/Chuck_Norris)

696.

Roderick Jaynes was nominated for Best Editing for "Fargo." Jaynes was not a real person, the name had been made up by the Coen brothers because they feel too vain listing their names so much in the credits. If asked about Jaynes, the Coen's say he is old and is too frail to attend events.

Reference: (https://en.wikipedia.org/wiki/Coen_brothers)

697.

The Rocky Mountain Locust once formed a swarm the size of California only to go extinct 30 years later.

Reference: (https://en.wikipedia.org/wiki/Rocky_Mountain_locust)

698.

Samsung helped teach an entire town sign language for a hearing impaired man, making him happy.

Reference: (https://youtu.be/UrvaSqN76h4)

699.

TV actors Debbie Allen and Phylicia Rashad are sisters.

Reference: (https://en.wikipedia.org/wiki/Debbie_Allen)

700.

Hummingbirds' metabolism rate is so high that they will starve to death in two hours if they don't eat.

Reference: (https://video.nationalgeographic.com/video/til/161021-sciex-til-anusha-shankar-hummingbirds)

701.

Kodak owned and operated a nuclear reactor in their Rochester, New York, facility complete with enriched uranium.

Reference: (https://gizmodo.com/5909961/kodak-had-a-secret-weapons-grade-nuclear-reactor-hidden-in-a-basement)

702.

In the Somerville Study, 500 juvenile criminals living in correctional facilities were given counselling, academic tutoring and psychiatric help. 30 years later, those who received help had higher rates of engagement in criminal activity when compared to the control group.

Reference: (https://en.wikipedia.org/wiki/Cambridge_Somerville_Youth_Study)

703.

The University of Texas spends an average of only $7.48 for every million gallons of water it consumes.

Reference: (https://utilities.utexas.edu/ut-austin-energy-data)

704.

Gamergate is a mated worker ant that is able to lay fertilized eggs that will develop as females.

Reference: (https://en.wikipedia.org/wiki/Gamergate)

705.

Of the top 10 nations that consume the most alcohol per capita in the world, 9 are either Russia or Eastern European. South Korea is the only Asian nation in the top 50, with the U.S. ranking 48. Ireland, U.K., Germany and Denmark drink nearly identical amounts per capita.

Reference:(https://en.wikipedia.org/wiki/List_of_countries_by_alcohol_consumption_per_capita#2010_WHO_data)

706.

"Bored of the Rings," published in 1969, is a parody of Lord of the Rings. Written by National Lampoon founder Douglas C. Kenney, it includes characters such as Frito Bugger and Goodgulf Grayteeth.

Reference: (https://en.wikipedia.org/wiki/Bored_of_the_Rings)

707.

Aviation pioneer Lawrence Sperry, the inventor of auto-pilot, also founded the Mile High Club.

Reference: (http://milehighclub.com/founding-member/)

708.

The Sears Max Axis Wrench is blatantly stolen from a small town inventor's adjustable wrench known as the "Bionic Wrench". After briefly selling the Bionic Wrench, Sears ripped off the idea and broke an agreement with the Bionic Wrench maker to make a clone wrench, a decision that cost $6 million dollars.

Reference: (http://www.ipwatchdog.com/2017/06/19/bionic-wrench-awarded-5-9m-sears-willful-infringement-verdict/id=84489/)

709.

The first Academy Awards took place on May 16th, 1929, at a private dinner held at the Hollywood Roosevelt Hotel in Los Angeles, California. Tickets cost $5, 270 people attended the event, and the presentation ceremony lasted 15 minutes.

Reference: (https://en.wikipedia.org/wiki/1st_Academy_Awards)

710.

Because rules for the 1984 Clio Awards, for advertising, required that a given entry appear publicly during the 1983 calendar year, Apple Computer's 1984 Macintosh Super Bowl commercial aired in December, 1983, on KMVT in Twin Falls, Idaho, after the normal sign-off.

Reference: (https://en.wikipedia.org/wiki/Clio_Awards#1980s)

711.

Before the Super Bowl XLI Halftime Show, the show coordinator asked Prince if he'd be alright performing in the downpour, to which Prince responded, "Can you make it rain harder?"

Reference: (https://www.youtube.com/watch?v=7NN3gsSf-Ys)

712.

One third of all motels in the U.S. are owned by Indians with the last name "Patel."

Reference: (https://nytimes.com/1999/07/04/magazine/a-patel-motel-cartel.html?referer=https://www.google.com/)

713.

Cough drops used to be made with morphine and heroin.

Reference: (https://en.wikipedia.org/wiki/Throat_lozenge#History)

714.

In 2012, Purina, a Nestle subsidiary, had to recall their Waggin Train Jerky treats after it was reported that an antibiotic in the product likely caused the death of hundreds of dogs in the U.S.

Reference: (http://www.dogsnaturallymagazine.com/purina-finally-recalls-waggin-train-and-canyon-creek-chicken-jerky-treats/)

715.

The world's first hard drive was larger than a refrigerator and could hold only 5 megabytes of storage.

Reference: (https://www.wired.com/2014/01/tech-time-warp-ibm-ramac/)

716.

In 2007, a man sued his doctor after a surgery gone wrong caused him to urinate feces and defecate urine.

Reference: (http://abcnews.go.com/Health/story?id=3935535)

717.

A British man tried to remove a wart by shooting it off with a shotgun. He succeeded in removing the wart but also shoot of his middle finger in the process.

Reference: (https://www.upi.com/Odd_News/2011/06/17/Man-shot-off-own-finger-to-get-rid-of-wart/UPI-54791308324840/)

718.

People who committed suicide in the Middle Ages were buried just outside of consecrated ground. The church went as far as to not even let the deceased pass over the grounds.

Reference: (https://www.prairieghosts.com/grave_history.html)

719.

In 1942, a Soviet submarine managed to sink a German transport ship with 2,000 Soviet prisoners of war onboard, killing them all, just for it to be sunk itself shortly afterwards.

Reference: (https://en.wikipedia.org/wiki/Battle_of_Cape_Burnas)

720.

Andy Bathgate was one of the first players to use a curved hockey stick. He broke the blade of his stick and noticed that when shooting, the puck moved erratically, making it harder for goalies to stop his shots.

Reference: (https://en.wikipedia.org/wiki/Ice_hockey_stick)

721.

In 1927, Firestone Tires were discovered to be using slave labor in Liberia by a joint League of Nations and United States of America investigation.

Reference: (https://www.jstor.org/stable/716534?seq=4#page_scan_tab_contents)

722.

The first type of cancer discovered was breast cancer, which was discovered in 1500 BC. The treatment back then was nearly the same as the treatment now, which was to just remove the tumor.

Reference: (https://www.ncbi.nlm.nih.gov/pmc/articles/PMC2927383/)

723.

Vitamin D can help the immune system fight cancer. It's essential to processes in both "innate" and "adaptive" immune cells, and appropriate supplementation may provide an anti-cancer boost.

Reference: (https://www.ncbi.nlm.nih.gov/pmc/articles/PMC1470481/)

724.

The "Mc" in Irish surnames means son and "O" means descendant.

Reference: (https://en.wikipedia.org/wiki/Irish_name#Surnames_and_prefixes)

725.

Terry Marsh legally changed his name to "None Of The Above X" and ran for parliament. He is also a professional chessboxer.

Reference: (https://en.wikipedia.org/wiki/Terry_Marsh_(boxer))

726.

Starting in 2011, Belgium went 535 days without a government.

Reference: (http://www.businessinsider.com/belgium-government-elio-di-rupo-2011-12#his-flemish-counterpart-bart-de-wever-is-head-of-the-n-va-7)

727.

The Sacred Band of Thebes were 300 elite soldiers made up of 150 pairs of male lovers. During the Battle of Chaeronia, they stood and fought to the death while their comrades ran. They were buried side by side.

Reference: (https://en.wikipedia.org/wiki/Sacred_Band_of_Thebes)

728.

Taiwanese garbage trucks are known to play music to encourage people to recycle.

Reference:(https://en.wikipedia.org/wiki/Waste_management_in_Taiwan#Waste_collection_and_disposal)

729.

Lepa Radic was caught by Nazis in World War II and refused to leak information at her execution. She told them that, "My comrades would reveal themselves when they avenge my death." At age 17, she was the youngest recipient of the posthumously issued Order of the People's Hero gallantry medal in Yugoslavia.

Reference: (https://en.wikipedia.org/wiki/Lepa_Radi%C4%87)

730.

Indonesia still has a monarchy in power within the country.

Reference: (https://en.wikipedia.org/wiki/Special_Region_of_Yogyakarta)

731.

The largest butterfly has a 12" wing span.

Reference: (https://www.mnn.com/earth-matters/animals/photos/10-of-the-largest-insects-in-the-world/queen-alexandras-birdwing)

732.

Some people like, French foreign minister Hubert Védrine, consider the United States a hyperpower, having eclipsed the status of a superpower.

Reference: (https://en.wikipedia.org/wiki/Hyperpower)

733.

Ypres, Belgium holds a cat-themed parade and festival to commemorate the medieval practice of throwing cats tied up in bags from tall buildings into the town square. In modern times, only plush toy cats are thrown, and are collected by an audience.

Reference: (https://en.wikipedia.org/wiki/Kattenstoet)

734.

Neil Armstrong's spacesuit was made by a bra manufacturer, Playtex.

Reference: (https://www.smithsonianmag.com/history/neil-armstrongs-spacesuit-was-made-by-a-bra-manufacturer-3652414/)

735.

The first steam powered airplane flew in 1848.

Reference: (https://en.wikipedia.org/wiki/John_Stringfellow)

736.

Africa is larger than Russia.

Reference: (https://en.wikipedia.org/wiki/Gall%E2%80%93Peters_projection)

737.

World War I was the first war in which mass media and propaganda played a significant role. It was one of the keys in convincing people to fight in the war. At the start of the war, the British cut Germany's undersea cables to influence the reporting of the war to the world.

Reference: (https://en.wikipedia.org/wiki/Propaganda_in_World_War_I)

738.

There is a Jewish myth about a giant lion called Tigris. The lion had a head that was 21 feet wide. In the myth, Tigris roared, women within 2,200 kilometers miscarried and a city was destroyed. Tigris roared a second time and the teeth of the men looking for Tigris fell out.

Reference: (https://en.wikipedia.org/wiki/Jewish_mythology)

739.

The MTA in New York City has two man teams that get dispatched to retrieve items that fall on the tracks.

Reference: (http://transittrax.mta.info/audio/ttx_transcpts/PlatformSafety.htm)

740.

Woodrow Wilson connected the Atlantic and Pacific Oceans via a telegraph that triggered the detonation of the last dam in the Panama Canal.

Reference:(https://en.wikipedia.org/wiki/Panama_Canal#George_Washington_Goethals_replaces_John_Frank_Stevens_as_chief_engineer)

741.

The name for the ITER project, an international fusion reactor, originally stood for International Thermonuclear Experimental Reactor but the long-form was dropped due to public concerns about the word "thermonuclear" used alongside "experimental". It now stands for "The Way" in Latin.

Reference: (https://en.wikipedia.org/wiki/ITER#Background)

742.

The Buddha had a mid-life crisis when he was 29 years old.

Reference: (http://interesting-facts.com/celebrity/buddhism-facts/#buddhism2)

743.

In 1967, Kathrine Switzer was the first woman to run the Boston marathon with an official number. After realizing that a woman was running, race organizer Jock Semple went after her trying to stop. The photographs taken of the incident made world headlines.

Reference: (https://en.wikipedia.org/wiki/Kathrine_Switzer)

744.

Most pistachios used to be dyed red, and would leave your hands and mouth with a red hue.

Reference: (https://www.huffingtonpost.com/entry/what-are-red-pistachios_n_6570944)

745.

Toyota sold a 3.5 V6 Corolla, the Blade Master-G.

Reference: (https://www.autocar.co.uk/car-review/toyota/auris/first-drives/toyota-blade-master-g)

746.

In 2013, we lost contact with the Deep Impact spacecraft due to a Y2K bug, even though it wasn't launched until 2005.

Reference: (https://news.nationalgeographic.com/news/2013/09/130920-deep-impact-ends-comet-mission-nasa-jpl/)

747.

Sari cloth is an effective way to remove cholera from drinking water. Filtering water to free it from microorganisms is practiced among Jains to follow the doctrine of nonviolence, preventing pain to any living creature.

Reference: (https://en.wikipedia.org/wiki/Cloth_filter)

748.

After David Bowie went to Bali with Iggy Pop, he was so impressed by the Balinese Cremation Ceremony that he requested he be transported back there upon his death and cremated in accordance with the Buddhist rituals of Bali. He ended up being cremated in New Jersey.

Reference: (https://www.nytimes.com/2016/01/30/nyregion/david-bowies-will-splits-estate-said-to-be-worth-100-million.html)

749.

In 1984, the New Zealand prime minister drunkenly called a general election and lost.

Reference: (https://en.wikipedia.org/wiki/New_Zealand_general_election,_1984#Background)

750.

The agency that handles North Korea's concentration camps is called the State Security Department.

Reference: (https://en.wikipedia.org/wiki/State_Security_Department)

751.

Cats were very revered in Ancient Egypt. A mob lynched a Roman for accidentally killing a cat even though the Pharaoh Ptolemy XII tried to dissuade them.

Reference: (https://en.wikipedia.org/wiki/Cats_in_ancient_Egypt#Cats_in_Egyptian_religion)

752.

Canada has a coin with a narwhal on it.

Reference: (http://www.mint.ca/store/coins/half-kilogram-fine-silver-coin-%E2%80%93-conservation-series-the-narwhal-%E2%80%93-mintage-500-2015-prod2530329)

753.

Self-flagellation was a religious movement in Europe in the 13th and 14th centuries, peaking during the Black Death. Flagellants even had their own songs.

Reference: (https://en.wikipedia.org/wiki/Geisslerlieder)

754.

Steinway & Sons pianos are handcrafted and take a year to build. The company's 600,000th piano was built in 2015 with an inlaid Fibonacci design in the lid. It is valued at $2.4 million.

Reference: (https://en.wikipedia.org/wiki/Steinway_%26_Sons)

755.

The Taa language is the language with the most distinct sounds, also called phonemes. While English, German and French all have around 40 phonemes, the Taa language has at least 93 different phonemes with many of those being variations of click sounds.

Reference: (https://en.wikipedia.org/wiki/Taa_language)

756.

In Hindu philosophy, there is no purpose in the creation of the Universe. All existence is the result of a "Divine or Creative Play" by Brahman.

Reference: (https://en.wikipedia.org/wiki/Lila_(Hinduism))

757.

The Outer Space Treaty forbids any nation from trying to own the Moon.

Reference: (https://en.wikipedia.org/wiki/Outer_Space_Treaty)

758.

April 15th is Steal Something from Work Day.

Reference: (https://stealfromwork.crimethinc.com/faq.html)

759.

Chicken wings, pizzas, and many other foods are legally sandwiches in Colorado.

Reference: (http://www.9news.com/mobile/article/news/local/a-lot-of-new-things-are-sandwiches-in-colorado/355383437)

760.

Execution by ritual torture was commonly carried out by Native tribes in northeastern United States and Canada. The torture could continue for days and was conducted publicly in the captors' village, where the entire population, including children, would watch and participate.

Reference: (https://en.wikipedia.org/wiki/Captives_in_American_Indian_Wars)

761.

When Millvina Dean, the last remaining survivor of the sinking of RMS Titanic, died, she was cremated, and her ashes were scattered from where the Titanic set sail.

Reference: (https://en.wikipedia.org/wiki/Millvina_Dean#Death)

762.

All alcoholic drinks sold in the United States are required to be mildly radioactive. If alcohol is made in a lab it won't have any radioactive signature but alcohol made from plants will always be slightly radioactive due to the background radiation in the air and ground

Reference; (https://gizmodo.com/yes-all-american-alcohol-has-to-be-radioactive-1770422846)

763.

The notion that NASA astronauts carry suicide pills for use in case they are marooned in outer space is untrue. Exposure to outer space results in a much faster and smoother demise compared to a suicide pill.

Reference: (https://www.realclearscience.com/blog/2013/10/astronauts-and-suicide-pills.html)

764.

Lemurs get high off large red millipedes by gently biting into them and making the millipede release a defensive toxin. They then spread this toxin through their fur and, thanks to the small concentration of cyanide within it, the lemurs enter a state of intoxication and salivate profusely.

Reference: (https://www.youtube.com/watch?v=Uis0boLNN8A&feature=youtu.be)

765.

K-DST, the classic rock radio station in the popular video game "Grand Theft Auto: San Andreas", was hosted by none other than Guns N' Roses frontman Axl Rose.

Reference: (http://gta.wikia.com/wiki/K-DST)

766.

A U.S. task force conducted one of the largest military disaster relief efforts ever carried out when they were coming back from the Gulf War but were diverted to Bangladesh to provide assistance during the aftermath of the 1991 Bangladesh tsunamis.

Reference: (https://en.wikipedia.org/wiki/1991_Bangladesh_cyclone#Operation_Sea_Angel)

767.

Steven Crowder worked as a voice actor for the character Alan "The Brain" Powers on the children's television series "Arthur."

Reference: (https://en.wikipedia.org/wiki/Steven_Crowder#Early_life_and_career)

768.

Drake's producer Noah "40" Shebib is in the movie "A Christmas Story". His mother is Miss Shields and she was pregnant with him during filming.

Reference: (https://www.nationalmssociety.org/Get-Involved/Personal-Stories/Ambassadors-Familiar-Faces/Noah-40-Shebib)

769.

Aurorae, namely Aurora Borealis or Aurora Australis, are actually plasma in the upper atmosphere.

Reference: (https://www.plasma-universe.com/Aurora)

770.

Major Digby Tatham-Warter was a British major who brought an umbrella into battle, using it to stop an armored vehicle by poking the driver's eye and saving a chaplain. When a fellow soldier complained about it, he answered, "oh my goodness, but what if it rains?"

Reference: (https://en.wikipedia.org/wiki/Digby_Tatham-Warter#Second_World_War)

771.

The United States Postmaster General is the second-highest paid U.S. government official, with a salary of $267,840, based on publicly available salary information, after the President of the United States.

Reference: (https://www.washingtontimes.com/news/2012/nov/15/us-postal-service-loses-159-billion/)

772.

In Asia, Jackie Chan promotes the George Foreman Grill.

Reference: (https://en.wikipedia.org/wiki/George_Foreman_Grill)

773.

Actress Sharon Stone was a bookworm and has a very high IQ.

Reference: (http://www.independent.co.uk/news/people/profiles/sharon-stone-interview-i-was-a-bookworm-i-used-my-intelligence-to-be-sexy-9338267.html)

774.

The first British satellite, Ariel 1, was nuked by the U.S.

Reference: (https://en.wikipedia.org/wiki/Ariel_1)

775.

The Yalu River Broken Bridge, which connected China and North Korea, was built by Japan and destroyed by the United States.

Reference: (https://en.wikipedia.org/wiki/Yalu_River_Broken_Bridge#history)

776.

The world record for a marathon World of Warcraft session is 29 hours.

Reference: (http://www.guinnessworldrecords.com/world-records/117415-longest-videogame-marathon-on-world-of-warcraft)

777.

Ortho-diethynylbenzene dianion is a superbase with a proton affinity of 1843 kJ mol−1, it has no known use.

Reference: (https://en.wikipedia.org/wiki/Ortho-diethynylbenzene_dianion)

778.

Sometimes humans regenerate fingertips if they're accidently amputated.

Reference: (https://www.npr.org/sections/health-shots/2013/06/10/190385484/chopped-how-amputated-fingertips-sometimes-grow-back)

779.

Colonoscopies carry a risk of explosions from flatulence gas in the intestine.

Reference: (https://io9.gizmodo.com/5945897/sometimes-people-explode-during-colonoscopies-heres-how-that-happens?IR=T)

780.

Photographer Melanie Willhide dedicated a series to a thief who stole her computer and corrupted her digital photographs by exhibiting those corrupted photographs.

Reference: (https://www.newyorker.com/culture/photo-booth/melanie-willhides-tribute-to-a-burglar)

781.

In China, drivers would rather kill you than injure you because if they injure you, they're liable for life.

Reference: (http://www.businessinsider.com/in-china-drivers-would-rather-kill-than-injure-2015-9)

782.

Actor John Posey originally played Danny Tanner in the unaired "Full House" pilot before being replaced by Bob Saget.

Reference: (https://www.youtube.com/watch?v=-qWZ9Hb6aKs)

783.

Louis Le Prince invented the "Motion Picture" three years before Thomas Edison, however, his mysterious disappearance erased him from the history books.

Reference: (https://en.wikipedia.org/wiki/Louis_Le_Prince)

784.

Approximately 1% of asthma cases in children are faked by their parents and caretakers in a form of Munchausen Syndrome by Proxy wherein a caretaker fakes an illness, usually in a child. This is typically done to gain attention and sympathy for themselves.

Reference: (http://adc.bmj.com/content/66/8/956.short)

785.

Hitler had his own dog killed so she wouldn't fall into the hands of the Russians. Her name was Blondi.

Reference: (https://en.wikipedia.org/wiki/Blondi)

786.

The man who invented Vaseline claimed to have eaten a spoonful of it every day. He lived to be 96.

Reference: (https://en.wikipedia.org/wiki/Robert_Chesebrough?4)

787.

The popular 1960's song "Bread and Butter" is not sung by a woman, but a very high pitched man.

Reference: (https://www.youtube.com/watch?v=-mx7vZDhStI)

788.

Whale flippers have skeletal structures that look like hands.

Reference: (http://www.ftexploring.com/askdrg/askdrgalapagos3.html)

789.

The theme song for the children's TV show Bob the Builder, "Can We Fix It?" was the biggest selling single of the year in 2000 in the U.K., appearing 80th in the all time U.K. best-sellers list and reached number one in Australia in 2001.

Reference: (https://en.wikipedia.org/wiki/Can_We_Fix_It%3F)

790.

In 2014, a German hacker managed to clone the fingerprint of the German defense minister, using nothing but pictures from a press event.

Reference: (http://www.bbc.com/news/technology-30623611)

791.

For 250 years, the rate of discovering new species is between 15,000 and 18,000 per year.

Reference: (https://www.atlasobscura.com/articles/new-animal-species)

792.

The Australian football team, Melbourne FC is the oldest professional football club in the world, being founded in 1859.

Reference: (https://en.wikipedia.org/wiki/Oldest_football_clubs#Before_1860)

793.

A dentist pulled 357 teeth in one day and then wore them as a necklace.

Reference: (http://www.oralanswers.com/what-happens-to-extracted-teeth/)

794.

Hot water can sometimes freeze quicker than cold water.

Reference: (https://en.wikipedia.org/wiki/Mpemba_effect)

795.

The popular 2000's song "Everytime We Touch" by Cascada is actually a cover of a song of the same name by Maggie Reilly.

Reference: (https://en.wikipedia.org/wiki/Everytime_We_Touch_(Maggie_Reilly_song))

796.

A Hollywood writer had a baby through a sperm donor, discovered her daughter has 15 half-brothers and sisters, contacted all of these families, and now they have dinner once a week and take vacations together.

Reference: (https://www.hollywoodreporter.com/news/23-hollywood-moms-same-sperm-763403)

797.

After the disastrous 2011 earthquake and tsunami in Japan, a disconnected telephone booth was set up in a town devastated by the tsunami so that relatives may "call" and say departing words to their lost loved ones.

Reference: (https://www.youtube.com/watch?v=ke-H5EEqvRs&feature=youtu.be)

798.

8 young adults in Oklahoma overdosed on a design drug in 2011. One member took the first dose to test it and once he starting feeling it the rest of the group took their dose. Minutes later the first man began to seize. Had the group waited 5 more minutes 2 of them would still be alive.

Reference: (https://www.erowid.org/experiences/exp.php?ID=92339)

799.

Until the invention of high speed photography in the 1870's, it wasn't known if horses lifted all four legs off the ground when galloping.

Reference: (https://en.wikipedia.org/wiki/Sallie_Gardner_at_a_Gallop)

800.

The city of Venice is built upon a foundation of thousands of tree trunks.

Reference: (https://www.youtube.com/watch?v=B3INp81NimE&feature=youtu.be)

801.

In order to popularize potatoes in Greece, Ioannis Kapodistrias placed armed guards around a potato shipment, while instructing the guards to turn a blind eye to theft.

Reference: (https://en.wikipedia.org/wiki/Ioannis_Kapodistrias)

802.

Cisco was named after the city of San Francisco and the logo is based off the Golden Gate Bridge.

Reference: (https://en.wikipedia.org/wiki/Cisco_Systems#/media/File:Cisco_logo.svg)

803.

The phrase "Lunatic Fringe" was originally just the name given circa 1875 to the fashion of cropping the hair and letting the ends hang down over the forehead.

Reference: (https://www.phrases.org.uk/meanings/lunatic-fringe.html)

804.

The Montana Highway Patrol patch has the symbol 3-7-77, which was once used to mark people's doors or tents informing them that they must leave town or end up on the receiving end of vigilantism.

Reference: (https://www.montanatrooper.com/3-7-77/)

805.

Blue only exists as a pigment in nature on one species of butterfly. All other blues in nature are the result of light refraction as opposed to pigment. In other words, nature and evolution solved a biological problem with microscopic engineering.

Reference: (https://www.npr.org/sections/health-shots/2014/11/12/347736896/how-animals-hacked-the-rainbow-and-got-stumped-on-blue)

806.

Carrie Anne Moss, Trinity from "The Matrix," was in a Canadian Show called "Matrix" that was released before the movie launched.

Reference: (https://en.wikipedia.org/wiki/Matrix_(TV_series))

807.

You are a "Jr." if you're named after your dad, but a "II" if you take the name from someone else in the family.

Reference: (http://www.differencebetween.net/miscellaneous/difference-between-jr-and-ii/)

808.

Pac-Man was originally going to be released in the U.S. as Puckman but the name was changed out of fears the "P" would be vandalized into another letter.

Reference: (https://www.wired.com/2010/05/pac-man-30-years/)

809.

Aphantasia is the inability to picture mental images or have a "mind's eye".

Reference: (https://en.wikipedia.org/wiki/Aphantasia)

810.

Leonardo DiCaprio surrendered Marlon Brando's Oscar and a Picasso piece over to the U.S. Government.

Reference: (http://www.latimes.com/entertainment/la-et-entertainment-news-updates-june-1497628778-htmlstory.html)

811.

Rodger Ebert wrote 3 screenplays for Russ Meyers.

Reference: (https://filmschoolrejects.com/27-things-learned-roger-eberts-beyond-valley-dolls-commentary/)

812.

The song "Puff the Magic Dragon" is not filled with drug references. The writer stated not to have known about marijuana when he wrote the song in 1958.

Reference: (http://www.songfacts.com/detail.php?id=1276)

813.

Even though physicists have confirmed every prediction made by the general relativity and quantum theories, they are mutually incompatible for very small or very massive objects. Therefore, a framework revealing a deeper underlying reality must be discovered in order to unify the two theories.

Reference: (https://en.wikipedia.org/wiki/Theory_of_everything)

814.

Women used to wear chameleons and other animals as jewelry. They would fasten chameleons to their hair and clothes, and admired how it changed colors to match their outfits.

Reference: (https://timeline.com/live-lizard-jewelry-history-b7569bb866f)

815.

A Gramogram is a letter or group of letters which can be pronounced to form one or more words, some examples include "XS" for "excess", "CU" for "see you", and "FUNEX" for "Have you any eggs?"

Reference: (https://en.wikipedia.org/wiki/Gramogram)

816.

A man under arrest used a handcuff key he had on a chain around his neck to free himself and grab a gun, killing 2 police officers and later a state trooper.

Reference: (https://en.wikipedia.org/wiki/Hank_Earl_Carr)

817.

There was once an underground network of pneumatic mail delivery tubes in New York City. Each tube could carry between 400 and 600 letters and traveled at 30 to 35 miles per hour.

Reference: (https://untappedcities.com/2013/03/15/nycs-pneumatic-tube-mail-network/)

818.

The USB symbol is modeled after the three-pronged trident that was carried by the Roman god of the sea, Neptune. It is supposed to represent power, and the shapes at the end of each spear tip represent the many devices a user can use with it.

Reference: (https://knowledgestew.com/2015/07/the-origins-of-7-common-symbols.html)

819.

Didier Delsalle is the only pilot to land a helicopter on the summit of Mount Everest at over 29,000 feet for nearly four minutes.

Reference: (https://www.verticalmag.com/features/landing-everest-didier-delsalle-recalls-record-flight/)

820.

A man survived 60 hours in an air pocket, in a sunken tug boat, 30 meters under water.

Reference: (http://www.cbc.ca/news/world/harrison-odjegba-okene-survived-3-days-in-air-bubble-under-water-1.2449565)

821.

There is a restaurant on the island of Lanzarote in which the food is cooked using the heat from a volcano. A large grill is balanced on basalt rocks built around the opening to a well of molten lava.

Reference: (https://www.atlasobscura.com/places/el-diablo-restaurant)

822.

A small portion of the ashes of Clyde Tombaugh, the person who discovered Pluto, is onboard the New Horizons probe.

Reference: (https://edition.cnn.com/2015/07/13/us/nasa-pluto-new-horizons-clyde-tombaugh-ashes/index.html)

823.

The phrases, "lock, stock, and barrel" and "cold shoulder", were both coined by Sir Walter Scott.

Reference: (https://en.wikipedia.org/wiki/Cold_shoulder)

824.

The U.S. Postal Service workers said they're being forced to fake package deliveries to make quota.

Reference: (https://www.aol.com/article/finance/2017/12/05/postal-workers-claim-theyre-being-forced-to-fake-package-delive/23298123/)

825.

Babu Chiri Sherpa spent 21 hours at the summit of Everest, which is a world record. Also, he did it without auxiliary oxygen.

Reference: (https://en.wikipedia.org/wiki/Babu_Chiri_Sherpa)

826.

A 72 year old health expert went on the Dick Cavitt Show and announced, "I've decided to live to be a hundred", then died minutes later on stage.

Reference: (https://nyti.ms/2ow9zv2)

827.

Tom Wilson, Biff from "Back to the Future," received the same questions about the movies so frequently, he made a song about them.

Reference: (https://www.youtube.com/watch?v=iwY5o2fsG7Y&feature=youtu.be)

828.

The "u" unit used to measure an atoms' mass is a Dalton, so, for instance, an atom weighing 1u is read "one Dalton" rather than "one unit" or "one u".

Reference: (https://en.wikipedia.org/wiki/Unified_atomic_mass_unit)

829.

Apart from being an animal right activist and vegetarian, Voltaire was very fond of Vedas and Hinduism.

Reference: (https://en.wikipedia.org/wiki/Voltaire#Hinduism)

830.

Beavers secrete a sort of anal-molasses that's used to make vanilla flavoring and scents.

Reference: (https://blog.nationalgeographic.org/2013/10/01/beaver-butts-emit-goo-used-for-vanilla-flavoring/)

831.

There is a recreational drug concoction called "Lean" which is made from cough syrup and soft drinks.

Reference: (https://drugabuse.com/library/lean-purple-drank/)

832.

In 1994, a 75 pound bale of cocaine was ejected from a smuggler plane by accident. The coke landed on the lawn of a house that was having its very first neighborhood crime watch meeting.

Reference: (https://www.deseretnews.com/article/392575/ONLY-IN-FLORIDA-DOES-COCAINE-DROP-FROM-SKY.html)

833.

McDonald's got rid of their small coffee stirring spoons because people were using them as cocaine spoons.

Reference: (https://www.snopes.com/fact-check/stirring-response/)

834.

The Hughes Memorial Tower is the tallest structure in Washington, D.C. It is over 200 feet taller than the Washington Monument.

Reference: (https://en.wikipedia.org/wiki/Hughes_Memorial_Tower)

835.

"Blowing a raspberry" comes from the Cockney rhyming slang for "fart," which is "raspberry tart," and "put up your dukes" comes from "Duke of York," rhyming slang for "fork," which itself was Cockney slang for "fist."

Reference: (https://en.wikipedia.org/wiki/Rhyming_slang#Development)

836.

The League of Extraordinary Communities, consists of Dull, in Scotland, Boring, in Oregon, United States, and Bland, in Australia.

Reference:(https://en.wikipedia.org/wiki/Dull,_Perth_and_Kinross#Paired_towns_(Twin_Towns))

837.

Chris Farley named his Matt Foley character after a friend who for a time lived in a van by a river. Matt is now a Catholic priest in Chicago.

Reference: (https://en.wikipedia.org/wiki/Chris_Farley)

838.

Hamilton Beach patented the first electric vibrator in 1902.

Reference: (http://www.vonnaharper.com/history-of-the-vibrator.html)

839.

Most beers couldn't withstand the 6 month trip from Great Britain to the British colonies in India, where the climate was too hot to brew. In response, a brewer heavily hopped and aged their beers, making them pale, and able to survive the journey.

Reference: (https://www.theguardian.com/lifeandstyle/2015/jan/30/brief-history-of-ipa-india-pale-ale-empire-drinks)

840.

Pete Rose was given the nickname "Charlie Hustle" by Yankees pitcher Whitey Ford after Rose sprinted to first base after a walk during a Spring Training game.

Reference: (https://en.wikipedia.org/wiki/Pete_Rose#Cincinnati_Reds_(1963%E2%80%9378))

841.

Director John Landis violated child labor laws and ignored warnings in a "Twilight Zone" scene with a helicopter and explosives. This resulted in the decapitation of Vic Morrow and a child actor, the death of another child actor, and the loss of the helicopter. He was acquitted of all charges.

Reference: (https://en.wikipedia.org/wiki/John_Landis#Twilight_Zone_deaths)

842.

Titanic's engines burned 600 tons of coal per day. 176 men worked around the clock to shovel it in by hand. 100 tons of ash was also ejected into the sea each day.

Reference: (https://en.wikipedia.org/wiki/RMS_Titanic#Power)

843.

Multi-grafted trees are fruit trees with different fruits from the same "family" grafted together on one tree.

Reference: (https://dengarden.com/gardening/plant-a-fruit-salad-tree-with-four-different-fruits-growing-in-same-tree)

844.

City lights close to beaches confuse baby tortoises as they hatch and dig out of the sand, making them walk away from the water and into the city.

Reference: (https://www.independent.co.uk/arts-entertainment/tv/news/planet-earth-2-ii-baby-turtle-hatchlings-scene-conservation-barbados-a7469316.html)

845.

25% of Africa is Nigerian, with Lagos being on track to become the third largest city in the world.

Reference: (http://worldpopulationreview.com/world-cities/lagos-population/)

846.

A Milwaukee man accused of stabbing his girlfriend and her daughter to death quoted Eminem's "Space Bound" to explain brutal crime.

Reference: (http://www.nydailynews.com/news/crime/milwaukee-man-quoted-eminem-song-explain-killing-girlfriend-article-1.3080496)

847.

Michael Myers' mask from Halloween was based on a Captain Kirk Halloween mask. William Shatner once went trick or treating in it with his kids.

Reference: (http://halloweendailynews.com/2015/03/william-shatner-trick-or-treats-as-michael-myers/)

848.

Upon hearing about the death of Teddy Roosevelt, Vice President Thomas R. Marshal declared, "death had to take him in his sleep, for if he was awake there'd have been a fight".

Reference: (https://en.wikiquote.org/wiki/Thomas_R._Marshall)

849.

There are around 22,426,000 Americans who make more than $100,000 a year.

Reference: (https://www.census.gov/data/tables/time-series/demo/income-poverty/cps-pinc/pinc-01.html)

850.

The Chinese UN Security Council Permanent seat was controlled by the Republic of China, or Taiwan, until 1971.

Reference: (https://en.wikipedia.org/wiki/China_and_the_United_Nations)

851.

Mummies are sometimes used in medicine to calibrate CAT scan machines.

Reference: (http://www.newworldencyclopedia.org/entry/Mummy)

852.

Edsger W. Dijkstra, the famous Dutch computer science pioneer, when asked about his job during his marriage rite in 1957, answered as "programmer" but the municipal authorities did not accept it on the grounds that there was no such profession.

Reference: (http://www.cs.utexas.edu/users/EWD/transcriptions/EWD03xx/EWD340.html)

853.

One reason Demi Moore got the role in "Ghost" is that she can produce tears from either eye on cue.

Reference: (https://www.vanityfair.com/hollywood/2015/07/ghost-pottery-scene-25th-anniversary)

854.

Lil' Wayne stole a sample from a South African artist, and with pending legal action, released the track to P2P networks.

Reference: (https://en.wikipedia.org/wiki/Karma-Ann_Swanepoel)

855.

The "Dementors", which were first introduced in "Harry Potter and The Prisoner Of Azkaban", represented J.K. Rowlings severe depression.

Reference: (http://news.bbc.co.uk/2/hi/entertainment/823330.stm)

856.

On the set of "Spider-Man: Homecoming," Michael Keaton would play pranks on Tom Holland by whispering "I'm Batman" during fight scenes.

Reference: (https://www.cinemablend.com/news/1614980/the-hilarious-way-michael-keaton-trolled-tom-holland-on-the-set-of-spider-man)

857.

The exhaust frequency of the Maserati Quattroporte is 333 HZ, which is a frequency level that supposedly stimulates the sexual arousal in women.

Reference: (https://www.factretriever.com/car-facts)

858.

Black and white film and TV created a higher percentage of people who dreamed in black and white. When film and TV became predominately color, it reverted back to a higher percentage dreaming in color again.

Reference: (https://www.telegraph.co.uk/news/science/science-news/3353504/Black-and-white-TV-generation-have-monochrome-dreams.html)

859.

Shrimp trawl fisheries catch 2% of the world total catch of all fish by weight, but produce more than one-third of the world total bycatch.

Reference: (https://en.wikipedia.org/wiki/Bycatch#Shrimp%20trawling)

860.

Being bitten by a human can be more dangerous than being bitten by a snake or a small animal. This is because there are at least 500 tribes of small organisms in each human mouth that can rapidly lead to severe infection.

Reference: (http://www.monitor.co.ug/Magazines/HealthLiving/689846-1169350-hm8it3z/index.html)

861.

Nobody younger than 29 years old ever won an Oscar for best actor in a leading role.

Reference:(https://en.wikipedia.org/wiki/List_of_oldest_and_youngest_Academy_Award_winners_and_nominees)

862.

The Leidenfrost Effect allows water to move up a grooved incline in a predictable direction.

Reference: (https://www.youtube.com/watch?v=zzKgnNGqxMw&feature=youtu.be)

863.

TGI Friday's began life as one of the first singles bars in New York City before becoming the restaurant chain it is today.

Reference: (https://en.wikipedia.org/wiki/T.G.I._Friday's)

864.

Peter the dolphin died of a broken heart after falling in love with a human.

Reference: (https://nypost.com/2014/06/10/the-dolphin-that-fell-in-love-with-a-human/)

865.

"The Dick Test" involves injecting the skin with 0.1 cubic centimeters of scarlet fever toxin to determine susceptibility to Scarlet Fever.

Reference: (https://www.britannica.com/science/Dick-test)

866.

Brinicle is super concentrated sea salt that falls from forming sea ice sheets. The falling salt has a much lower freezing point that water, instantly freezing all water it touches and kills any living thing it touches.

Reference: (https://www.youtube.com/watch?v=1AupJzH31tc&feature=youtu.be)

867.

The oldest naval ship still in commission is HMS Victory. She was launched in 1765.

Reference: (https://en.wikipedia.org/wiki/HMS_Victory)

868.

There is a genetic condition which gives people increased muscle strength and twice the usual amount of muscle mass. There are no known related health issues. Affected people are intellectually normal.

Reference: (https://en.wikipedia.org/wiki/Myostatin-related_muscle_hypertrophy)

869.

Milky Way obstructs our view of around 20% of the extragalactic sky at visible wavelengths. That area is called the Zone of Avoidance and it is the reason humans do not have a complete picture of the extragalactic sky yet.

Reference: (https://en.wikipedia.org/wiki/Zone_of_Avoidance)

870.

Elmer Edward Solly assumed rock and roll group Sha Na Na's lead guitarist Vinnie Taylor's identity after Taylor died of a drug overdose. Solly was an escaped child killer, and by performing as Taylor, eventually led to Solly's discovery and capture.

Reference: (https://en.wikipedia.org/wiki/Sha_Na_Na#Member_information)

871.

The first recorded incident of streaking is when a man was arrested for running naked in London in 1799, when he accepted a wager of ten guineas to run from Cornhill to Cheapside.

Reference: (https://en.wikipedia.org/wiki/Streaking#History)

872.

OSCAR-7, an amateur radio satellite launched in 1974 and thought to have failed in 1981, allowed Polish anti-communist activists to safely and clandestinely communicate when martial law was imposed. The telephone network had been shuttered, and other communications methods too easily discovered.

Reference: (https://en.wikipedia.org/wiki/AMSAT-OSCAR_7)

873.

Russia was the first country to introduce decimal currency in 1704.

Reference: (https://en.wikipedia.org/wiki/Decimalisation)

874.

Street artist Banksy was the goalkeeper for a British soccer team; he even traveled to Mexico with the team.

Reference: (http://www.bbc.com/news/uk-england-bristol-19410566)

875.

The Vasa, built in 1628 as the flagship of the Swedish fleet, sank a kilometer into its maiden voyage in sight of thousands of well-wishers.

Reference: (https://en.wikipedia.org/wiki/Vasa_(ship)#Maiden_voyage)

876.

In 1987, Apple released a concept video for technology in 2011 featuring a tablet computer named "The Knowledge Navigator" with a voice parsing assistant. In 2011, Apple released Siri.

Reference: (https://www.youtube.com/watch?v=umJsITGzXd0)

877.

During the Indian and Pakistan partition, whole villages, small towns and parts of cities moved across borders. The communities often kept the same name they used previously; this has led to many places having the same name in both countries.

Reference: (http://www.freepressjournal.in/topic/cities-with-same-name-in-india-and-pakistan)

878.

When Jim Carrey played Andy Kaufman in "Man on the Moon" he was method acting. He did such a good job that when Andy Kaufman's sister visited the set, she believed Jim Carrey was a "vessel" which allowed Andy to communicate from beyond the grave and talk to his sister.

Reference: (http://www.newsweek.com/2017/12/01/andy-kaufman-jim-carrey-netflix-tony-clifton-713959.html)

879.

Submarine pioneer John Philip Holland was really called Seán Pilib Ó hUallacháin. He came from an Irish-speaking family in County Clare and didn't speak English until his teens.

Reference: (https://en.wikipedia.org/wiki/John_Philip_Holland)

880.

The 1986s "Howard the Duck" box office failure lead the film's producer, George Lucas, to be so badly in debt that he had to sell the just-launched computer-animation division to his friend, Steve Jobs of Apple. That same year, Jobs renamed the company to Pixar.

Reference: (https://www.bathroomreader.com/2013/08/fabulous-flop-how-howard-the-duck-changed-hollywood/)

881.

Warfarin, a blood thinning agent taken by more than 20 million Americans, is rat poison.

Reference: (https://www.nature.com/articles/nrcardio.2017.172)

882.

For the production of the epic 1970 movie "Waterloo", approximately 17,000 real soldiers were used as extras. They were provided by the Soviet Union, which partly financed the film.

Reference: (https://www.theguardian.com/film/2009/sep/10/waterloo-orson-welles-reel-history)

883.

Saint Patrick was not actually Irish.

Reference: (http://time.com/4261456/st-patrick-day-2016-history-real-saint/)

884.

A 3 mile journey on a steam train, which would have taken 1,000 gallons of water and a ton of coal, can be replaced by a diesel engine burning 18 gallons of fuel; that's a 98% fall in energy use between the two technologies.

Reference:(https://en.wikipedia.org/wiki/Mount_Washington_Cog_Railway#Environmental_concerns)

885.

The code-name for Winston Churchill's funeral procession was called "Operation Hope Not".

Reference: (https://en.wikipedia.org/wiki/Operation_Hope_Not)

886.

When Rear Admiral Cockburn led the burning of Washington during the War of 1812, American newspapers contemptuously nicknamed him "The Ruffian".

Reference:(https://en.wikipedia.org/wiki/Burning_of_Washington#Other_Washington_properties)

887.

The St. Patrick's Day tradition of dyeing the Chicago River green arose by accident when a group of plumbers used green dye to trace illegal substances that were polluting the river. The dyeing of the river is still sponsored by the local plumbers union.

Reference: (https://en.wikipedia.org/wiki/Chicago_River#St._Patrick's_Day)

888.

In the early 2000s, U.S. officials mulled shooting down the European Union's Galileo navigation satellites during a conflict because the frequencies they planned to operate on are more accurate than GPS. Concern was heightened when the Chinese showed interest in the project's capabilities.

Reference:(https://en.wikipedia.org/wiki/Galileo_(satellite_navigation)#Tension_with_the_United_States)

889.

Robert Williams, a Ford assembly line worker, is the first human in history to have been killed by a robot. He was hit by a robotic arm in 1979.

Reference: (https://www.wired.com/2010/01/0125robot-kills-worker/)

890.

Alessandro Moreschi was a castrato singer of the late 19th century and the only castrato to make solo recordings.

Reference: (https://www.youtube.com/watch?v=KLjvfqnD0ws)

891.

The flushing power of a toilet is measured by the number of grams of miso it can successfully flush.

Reference: (http://www.map-testing.com/performance-toilets-testing/)

892.

Radithor was a radioactive drink that was a quack cure and led to the death of Eben Byers, who consumed 3 bottles of it a day for 2 years until his teeth fell out and his bones began to degrade.

Reference: (https://www.orau.org/ptp/collection/quackcures/radith.htm)

893.

There is a bridge in Durham, North Carolina, that has been the cause of over 100 crashes in the past 10 years.

Reference: (https://www.nbcnews.com/nightly-news/north-carolina-can-opener-bridge-continues-wreak-havoc-trucks-n492511)

894.

The guns on the HMS Belfast, the battleship moored on the Thames, are aimed at a service station in North London.

Reference: (https://londonist.com/2015/02/why-do-the-guns-of-hms-belfast-point-at-a-motorway-service-station)

895.

The official color of Ireland is not green, but St. Patrick's blue.

Reference: (https://en.wikipedia.org/wiki/St._Patrick%27s_blue)

896.

March 17 is not only Saint Patrick's Day, it's also Saint Gertrude of Neville's Day. She's the patron saint of cats and cat lovers.

Reference: (https://en.wikipedia.org/wiki/Gertrude_of_Nivelles)

897.

Right before launching the two Voyagers, NASA scientists used kitchen-grade aluminum foil to cover critical parts of the probes to protect it from unanticipated radiation on Jupiter. It worked.

Reference: (http://www.businessinsider.com/voyager-kitchen-aluminum-wrap-radiation-short-circuit-2017-9)

898.

1 in 50 people have a brain aneurysm that has not yet ruptured.

Reference: (https://www.bafound.org/about-brain-aneurysms/brain-aneurysm-basics/brain-aneurysm-statistics-and-facts/)

899.

Until 1961, pubs in Ireland were not allowed to open on St. Patrick's Day.

Reference:(http://content.time.com/time/specials/packages/article/0,28804,1972553_1972551_1972550,00.html)

900.

If you smell a natural gas leak, you should not turn off a light switch as it creates a spark.

Reference: (https://www.npower.com/home/help-and-support/emergency-information/gas-safety-advice/gas-leaks/)

901.

The 1932 Winter Olympics, in Lake Placid, featured a live band on the ice that provided the music for figure skaters to perform to.

Reference: (https://www.youtube.com/watch?v=2ZLU-NhDfBU)

902.

The Chipko Movement started in India in 1730, with 363 villagers sacrificing their lives by hugging the trees to protect them from the foresters.

Reference: (https://en.wikipedia.org/wiki/Chipko_movement)

903.

Pigasus was a pig nominated for U.S. Presidency in 1968. The anti-war activists responsible demanded treatment as candidate, including security and access to briefings. Pigasus and his team were finally arrested during a "rally" and charged with disturbing the peace and bringing a pig to Chicago.

Reference: (https://actipedia.org/project/pigasus-president)

904.

Before forming The White Stripes, Jack White worked as an upholsterer. Here he hid 100 vinyl copies of his then-band The Upholsterers' records by stitching them into furniture. As of 2014, only two copies had been discovered.

Reference: (https://www.theguardian.com/music/2014/dec/19/jack-white-upholsterers-7-inch-found-furniture?CMP=Share_iOSApp_Other)

905.

Some turtles can breathe through their anuses.

Reference: (https://www.straightdope.com/columns/read/2325/is-it-true-turtles-breathe-through-their-butts/)

906.

The Japanese have a Honen Matsuri Festival for fertility where a giant phallus is paraded through the town.

Reference: (https://www.japan-experience.com/city-nagoya/honen-matsuri)

907.

McDonald's once made broccoli that tastes like bubblegum.

Reference: (http://www.businessinsider.com/mcdonalds-bubble-gum-broccoli-2014-11)

908.

British actor Gareth Jones died of a heart attack while performing in a live televised play in 1958, in which his character was scripted to have a heart attack. The rest of the cast improvised around his death and finished the play.

Reference: (https://www.theguardian.com/culture/2009/may/31/television-drama-theatre)

909.

There are pieces of Beethoven's skull at San Jose State University's Ira F. Brilliant Center for Beethoven Studies.

Reference: (https://www.funeralwise.com/digital-dying/how-beethovens-skull-got-to-san-jose/)

910.

Traditionally Chinese was written from right to left in vertical columns. Since 1949, horizontal writing has become the standard in mainland China, and all PRC newspapers changed from vertical to horizontal text in 1956.

Reference: (https://www.omniglot.com/chinese/structure.htm)

911.

Bhang is an edible preparation of cannabis. It was used in food and drink as early as 1000 B.C. in the Indian subcontinent.

Reference: (https://en.wikipedia.org/wiki/Bhang)

912.

The "Walk of Shame" from "Game of Thrones" was an actual ritual commonly practiced in Europe called "Skimmington", "Charivari" or "Rough Music" in England, to socially punish or shame individuals.

Reference: (https://en.wikipedia.org/wiki/Charivari)

913.

U.S. President Martin van Buren received a pair of tiger cubs as a gift from the Sultan of Oman. President Van Buren wanted to keep the cubs, but Congress insisted they belonged to the people. Eventually the president donated the tigers to the zoo.

Reference: (http://ourwhitehouse.org/lions-and-tigers-and-bear-oh-my-wild-animals-at-the-white-house/)

914.

Kobe Bryant speaks fluent Italian.

Reference: (https://www.youtube.com/watch?v=kwkMf6R3qSA)

915.

St. Patrick's birth name was Maewyn Succat.

Reference: (https://www.awesomestories.com/asset/view/MAEWYN-SUCCAT-KIDNAPPING-VICTIM-St.-Patrick-of-St.-Patrick-s-Day)

916.

10 years before Americans landed on the Moon, in 1959, the USSR intentionally crashed the Luna 2 probe on the Moon, carrying a ball made up of pentagonal Soviet pennants, which were released onto the lunar surface when the ball exploded upon landing.

Reference: (http://mentalfloss.com/article/94155/1959-soviets-littered-moon-tiny-metal-pennants)

917.

Damnatio memoriae is a Roman dishonor that intended to erase traitors from history.

Reference: (https://en.wikipedia.org/wiki/Damnatio_memoriae)

918.

The world's oldest continuously operating amusement park is in Denmark, and has been open since 1583.

Reference: (http://www.guinnessworldrecords.com/world-records/oldest-amusement-park-in-operation)

919.

In 1990, NBC's fall lineup included the much anticipated "Ferris Bueller's Day Off" television show as the lead in to another new show, "The Fresh Prince of Bel Air." "Ferris Bueller's Day Off" didn't last the season and was cancelled after 13 episodes.

Reference: (https://www.tvobscurities.com/articles/ferris_bueller/)

920.

Sonic The Hedgehog's sidekick Miles "Tails" Prower was based on a Kitsune, a creature from Japanese folklore that could grow multiple tails over time.

Reference: (https://en.wikipedia.org/wiki/Tails_(character))

921.

The United States hasn't completely banned asbestos. Certain products containing asbestos are still legal, like clothing and preformed building products. The EPA tried to ban almost all asbestos products in 1989, but the Fifth Circuit Court of Appeals overturned the ban in 1991.

Reference: (https://www.epa.gov/asbestos/us-federal-bans-asbestos)

922.

The largest youth organization in the USA is the National FFA Organization, with over 600,000 student members. It is an organization based on middle school and high school classes that promote agricultural education.

Reference: (https://en.wikipedia.org/wiki/National_FFA_Organization)

923.

The site where Julius Caesar was assassinated, the east portico of the Theater of Pompey in the Campus Martius in Rome, is now called the Torre Argentina and now operates as a sanctuary for stray cats.

Reference: (http://honesttopaws.com/rome-cat-sanctuary/)

924.

The U.S. doesn't actually use the "Imperial system" of units but instead the "U.S. customary system" which has slight differences to the Imperial system mostly used in the U.K.

Reference: (https://en.wikipedia.org/wiki/United_States_customary_units)

925.

Shaquille O'Neal is an honorary U.S. Deputy Marshall, and holds the record for tallest Sheriff's Deputy in the U.S.

Reference: (http://www.macon.com/news/local/article118974838.html)

926.

The most common song Rush played live was Neil Peart performing a drum solo, which he did over 1,500 times in his career, beating out their second most performed song by nearly 200 performances.

Reference: (https://www.setlist.fm/stats/rush-13d6dd1d.html)

927.

Ruts leftover from the wagon trains traveling the Oregon Trial, are still visible today.

Reference: (https://www.smithsonianmag.com/travel/follow-relics-oregon-trail-180960589/)

928.

The skull the Russians used to prove Hitler's death is actually the skull of a woman.

Reference: (https://amp.theguardian.com/world/2009/sep/27/adolf-hitler-suicide-skull-fragment)

929.

The U.K. edition vinyl album cover of "The White Stripes' Elephant" was made from recycled elephant dung.

Reference: (http://www.nme.com/news/music/the-white-stripes-11-1244850)

930.

The United States and North Korea were both on the same side in the Third Indochina War, supporting the efforts of various Communist forces fighting Soviet-backed Vietnamese aggression, following the departure of American forces after the Second Indochina War.

Reference: (https://en.wikipedia.org/wiki/Third_Indochina_War)

931.

In the 1983 movie "WarGames", John Lennon was interested in playing the character of Dr. Stephen Falken, but was murdered while the script was still in development.

Reference: (https://en.wikipedia.org/wiki/WarGames)

932.

Genie was a feral child who was strapped to a potty chair for 13 years of her life, deprived of human interaction and never gained the proper ability of language.

Reference: (https://www.theguardian.com/society/2016/jul/14/genie-feral-child-los-angeles-researchers)

933.

A Peanuts fan song appeared at number 2 on the Billboard charts during the week of December 31st, 1966. The song was unauthorized at first but eventually Charles Schulz let them continue to write Snoopy songs.

Reference: (https://en.wikipedia.org/wiki/Snoopy_vs._the_Red_Baron_(song))

934.

GM produced an Electric Pickup during the same period as their EV1 cars that utilized the same infrastructure, yet many trucks remain in use today while the fleet life of many of these ended in 2007 and 2008.

Reference: (https://en.wikipedia.org/wiki/Chevrolet_S-10_EV)

935.

On May 1st, 1969, Fred Rogers appeared before the U.S. Senate Commerce Committee requesting funds to help support the growth of a new concept, National Public Television.

Reference: (https://youtu.be/fKy7ljRr0AA)

936.

A very common group of pesticides, Organophosphates, are nerve agents.

Reference: (https://en.wikipedia.org/wiki/Organophosphate)

937.

Boxed wine was invented in 1935, based on a bag inside a box used by mechanics to hold and transport battery acid.

Reference: (https://en.wikipedia.org/wiki/Box_wine#History)

938.

Lorenzo Music, the voice of Garfield, would volunteer at a suicide hotline. Callers would sometimes change their tone to remark, "Hey, you sound just like that cat on TV!"

Reference: (https://www.newsfromme.com/2001/08/05/lorenzo-music-r-i-p/)

939.

In 2004, while searching the Paris Catacombs, police discovered a cinema in one of the caverns. It was equipped with a giant screen, seats for the audience, a fully stocked bar, and a complete restaurant. The source of its electrical power and the identity of those responsible remain unknown.

Reference: (https://www.theguardian.com/world/2004/sep/08/filmnews.france)

940.

Herbivores are opportunistic predators of smaller animals.

Reference: (https://www.smithsonianmag.com/smart-news/when-herbivores-arent-poor-chicken-got-eaten-cow-180951115/)

941.

There's a special font for people with dyslexia that makes it easier for them to read.

Reference: (https://www.dyslexiefont.com/en/typeface/)

942.

At the age of 21, Bill Pullman suffered a head injury and lost his sense of smell.

Reference: (http://www.contactmusic.com/bill-pullman/news/movie-wine-buff-pullman-has-no-sense-of-smell_1122513)

943.

The Denmark Strait isn't near Denmark.

Reference: (https://wikipedia.org/wiki/Denmark_Strait)

944.

If you find a four leaf clover, chances are good you will find more in the near vicinity.

Reference: (https://www.wired.com/2015/03/mysterious-genetics-four-leaf-clover/)

945.

St. Patrick was not Irish but, as a teen, was kidnapped by pirates and sold into slavery in Ireland to herd and tend sheep.

Reference: (http://www.saintpatricksdayparade.com/life_of_saint_patrick.htm)

946.

The famous Red Phone, the direct line connecting Washington and Moscow, has never been neither red nor a phone. The Red Phone is a notion created by pop culture.

Reference: (https://en.wikipedia.org/wiki/Moscow%E2%80%93Washington_hotline)

947.

The United States used a submarine in 1776, during the American Revolutionary War, to plant an underwater bomb on a British warship. Though unsuccessful, this was the first time a submarine had been used in naval warfare.

Reference: (https://www.history.com/this-day-in-history/worlds-first-submarine-attack)

948.

Eminem was offered the lead role in the 2013 science-fiction film "Elysium," but he turned it down because director Neill Blomkamp would not change its location from Los Angeles to Detroit.

Reference: (https://www.theguardian.com/music/2013/jul/18/eminem-di-antwoord-ninja-elysium)

949.

Months after the Saturday Night Massacre, President Nixon blamed the media, establishment, partisans and the special prosecutor's staff for trying to take him down, and still had many supporters.

Reference: (https://www.nytimes.com/1974/07/21/archives/mr-nixons-supporters-dont-take-it-quietly-aides-and-outsiders-damn.html)

950.

One of the biggest sound systems dubbed "The Wall of Sound" was made with 604 speakers for Grateful Dead.

Reference: (https://en.wikipedia.org/wiki/Wall_of_Sound_(Grateful_Dead))

951.

In 1958, a giant panda named Chi Chi was denied entry to the U.S. because she was a resident of Communist China.

Reference: (https://www.cia.gov/news-information/featured-story-archive/2015-featured-story-archive/panda-diplomacy.html)

952.

John Peel played The Undertones "Teenage Kicks" twice in a row when he first aired the song on his radio show, because he loved it so much. He later had the song played at his funeral, and had the lyric, "Teenage dreams, so hard to beat", written on his gravestone.

Reference: (https://www.youtube.com/watch?v=ZPzyN8Qq5XA)

953.

Many shoe stores in the U.S. during the 1940's and 1970's had shoe-fitting fluoroscopes, which were essentially X-ray machines for the feet to see how well a person's foot fit in the shoes they were considering buying.

Reference: (https://gizmodo.com/the-insane-cancer-machines-that-used-to-live-in-shoe-st-789073694)

954.

Big law staff lawyers can earn bonuses of $100,000 to $400,000 per year.

Reference: (https://abovethelaw.com/2017/12/associate-compensation-scorecard-2017-which-firms-have-announced-bonuses/)

955.

The surnames "Butt" and "Butts" are old occupational surnames originating from the Middle English term "But" meaning an archery target, implying that the first familial ancestors with the surname had an occupation in archery.

Reference: (https://en.wikipedia.org/wiki/Butt_(name))

956.

Stephen Fry was under criminal investigation in 2017 for blasphemy, for his comments made on the show "The Meaning of Life".

Reference: (https://www.independent.ie/irish-news/stephen-fry-blasphemy-probe-dropped-after-garda-fail-to-find-substantial-number-of-outraged-people-35692915.html)

957.

Because cows have 4 distinct stomach chambers, there are four distinct types of tripe: blanket, honeycomb, book, and reed.

Reference: (https://en.wikipedia.org/wiki/Tripe)

958.

Sweetwater, Florida was founded by retired "Russian Circus Midgets".

Reference: (http://www.miamiherald.com/news/local/community/miami-dade/west-miami-dade/article4453739.html)

959.

At the end of the extended edition of "Lord Of The Rings: The Fellowship Of The Ring," every single member of The Lord Of The Rings Official Fan Club that donated to the production of the film is thanked, adding an additional twenty minutes to the run time.

Reference: (http://lotr.wikia.com/wiki/The_Lord_of_the_Rings_Extended_Edition)

960.

Babies who are exposed to a certain food in the womb are more likely to enjoy the same food once born.

Reference: (https://www.ncbi.nlm.nih.gov/pmc/articles/PMC1351272/)

961.

Samose was the first Native American to make contact with the Pilgrims of Plymouth Colony. He entered the settlement unannounced, greeted the colonists in English, which he had learned from fishermen in Maine, and asked for beer.

Reference: (https://en.wikipedia.org/wiki/Samoset)

962.

An amateur astronomer was able to take detailed pictures of a secret military KH-12 spy satellite in orbit, from his backyard.

Reference: (http://www.spacesafetymagazine.com/space-debris/astrophotography/view-keyhole-satellite/)

963.

A British fertility doctor impregnated women with his own sperm 600 times.

Reference: (https://www.telegraph.co.uk/news/9193014/British-man-fathered-600-children-at-own-fertility-clinic.html)

964.

Erik Weihenmayer is a blind rock climber who uses prosthetic "eyes" that translate images to electrical impulses he feels on his tongue.

Reference: (http://discovermagazine.com/2008/jul/23-the-blind-climber-who-sees-through-his-tongue)

965.

Oscypek is a smoked cheese made of sheep milk exclusively in the Tatra Mountains region of Poland.

Reference: (https://en.wikipedia.org/wiki/Oscypek)

966.

In 2000, Coca-Cola launched a campaign against water called H2NO, in which the program taught waiters how to use "suggestive selling techniques" to offer a variety of alternative beverages when diners asked for water.

Reference: (https://en.wikipedia.org/wiki/H2NO)

967.

Chickenpox and shingles are caused by a herpes-like virus.

Reference: (https://en.wikipedia.org/wiki/Varicella_zoster_virus)

968.

The Verrazano-Narrows Bridge, which connects Staten Island to Brooklyn, was named for Italian explorer Giovanni da Verrazzano, but due to a mistake in naming, only has one "z" instead of two.

Reference: (https://en.wikipedia.org/wiki/Verrazano-Narrows_Bridge)

969.

In the late 1700s and 1800s, there was widespread panic about the evils of book-reading, which was described as, "an outrage on decency and common sense". People were concerned that avid novel-readers were "addicted" and were becoming anti-social.

Reference: (https://timeline.com/what-technology-are-we-addicted-to-this-time-f0f7860f2fab)

970.

In 1980, punk rock band Dead Kennedys was invited to play at an awards show to give the event "new wave credibility". Seconds into their set, they stopped to perform "Pull My Strings", a song written specifically to take the piss out of the music executives in the room. They never played it again.

Reference: (https://davesstrangeworld.com/2014/05/12/pull-my-strings-the-dead-kennedys/)

971.

The Nazi "perfect Aryan" poster child was Jewish.

Reference: (https://www.telegraph.co.uk/news/worldnews/europe/germany/10938062/Nazi-perfect-Aryan-poster-child-was-Jewish.html)

972.

Modern hybridization of roses through artificial, controlled pollination began with the horticulturalist of Empress Joséphine, the first wife of Napoleon, Andre Dupont. Prior to this, most new rose cultivars were spontaneous mutations or accidental, bee-induced hybrids, and appeared rarely.

Reference: (https://en.wikipedia.org/wiki/Empress_Jos%C3%A9phine)

973.

In 2003, Kees Moeliker was awarded the Ig Nobel Prize, a parody of the Nobel Prize, for his study of homosexual necrophilia in male mallard ducks.

Reference: (https://en.wikipedia.org/wiki/List_of_Ig_Nobel_Prize_winners)

974.

Munster Rugby is the first Irish team, including the Irish National Team, to beat the All Blacks in a competitive match in 1978.

Reference:(https://en.wikipedia.org/wiki/History_of_rugby_union_matches_between_Munster_and_New_Zealand#2008)

975.

Jewish Nobel Prize Winner Isaac Bashevis Singer, who fled Poland because of the Nazi threat in the 1930s, wrote that, "In relation to animals, all people are Nazis; for the animals, it is an eternal Treblinka."

Reference: (https://en.wikipedia.org/wiki/Animal_rights_and_the_Holocaust#cite_note-Patterson-3)

976.

In Kenya, elephant dung is being used to make paper. Elephants defecate up to 50 kilograms per day, which can produce 125 sheets of paper. This helps save the indigenous tree population and forest from being destroyed, along with creating a need for the 7,000 elephants left in Kenya.

Reference: (http://www.bbc.com/news/business-36162953)

977.

Tobacco smoke contains a radioactive chemical element called polonium-210. Polonium is a highly radioactive chemical with no stable isotopes.

Reference: (http://www.healthydietbase.com/the-hidden-danger-of-radioactive-polonium-in-tobacco/)

978.

Vanilla Ice wrote his famous "Ninja Rap" song for "Teenage Mutant Ninja Turtles: The Secret of the Ooze" in 30 minutes on an SP 1200 drum machine while in his hotel room.

Reference: (http://www.mtv.com/news/1890245/vanilla-ice-ninja-rap-interview/)

979.

"Urchin" is just another word for hedgehog, which is where sea urchins get their name. They are hedgehogs of the sea.

Reference: (https://en.wikipedia.org/wiki/Sea_urchin)

980.

Joseph Priestley discovered the existence of oxygen but never believed it played any part in combustion.

Reference: (https://en.wikipedia.org/wiki/Joseph_Priestley)

981.

The state of Florida does not allow married couples to divorce while one of the partners is pregnant.

Reference: (http://blog.cjamiesonlaw.com/can-i-get-a-divorce-in-florida-while-pregnant)

982.

David Bowie had to cancel an idea for his 1990 greatest hits tour that would let fans vote for the songs that would be played after the NME ran a campaign to try and force him to play "The Laughing Gnome," a novelty song he made before he was famous.

Reference: (https://en.wikipedia.org/wiki/The_Laughing_Gnome)

983.

Two orphaned human embryos went up for adoption after their biological parents died in a plane crash.

Reference: (http://articles.latimes.com/1987-12-04/news/mn-17700_1_embryos-frozen-couples)

984.

Rotten and pocket boroughs in the U.K. were ones where the patron of a parliamentary candidate could ensure his election because the borough's population was, respectively, disproportionately small due to the decline of the borough, or entirely beholden to a single landlord for shelter.

Reference: (https://en.wikipedia.org/wiki/Rotten_and_pocket_boroughs)

985.

Letters addressed to God in Israel are taken to the Western Wall in Jerusalem and placed in the cracks of the wall in a festival ceremony once a year.

Reference: (https://www.telegraph.co.uk/news/newstopics/howaboutthat/3708519/Letters-written-to-God-are-delivered-to-the-cracks-in-Jerusalems-Wailing-Wall.html)

986.

Rain is dirty. Apparently, winds carry dust particles into the atmosphere where they get covered with water vapor and fall to the ground as raindrops when storm clouds form.

Reference: (https://physics.aps.org/story/v7/st14)

987.

While imprisoned for murdering 7 people in Australia, Ivan Milat "The Backpacker Killer" cut off his little finger with a plastic knife in 2011 in order to send it by mail to the High Court of Australia.

Reference: (https://en.wikipedia.org/wiki/Backpacker_murders)

988.

There are nine subspecies of giraffes that are distinguishable by their pattern.

Reference: (https://giraffeconservation.org/giraffe-species/)

989.

Brad Pitt believes he has Prosopagnosia or "face blindness", a condition in which he has trouble recognizing and remembering faces, including his own.

Reference: (http://www.medicaldaily.com/brad-pitt-says-he-has-face-blindness-prosopagnosia-more-common-thought-246184)

990.

Star India, one of India's largest media conglomerates, is a fully owned subsidiary of 21st Century Fox.

Reference: (https://en.wikipedia.org/wiki/Star_India)

991.

Edvard Munch described his inspiration for "The Scream" as follows: "I was walking along a path, the city on one side and the fjord below. The Sun was setting, the clouds turning blood red. I sensed a scream passing through nature. I painted the clouds as actual blood. This became The Scream".

Reference: (https://en.wikipedia.org/wiki/The_Scream)

992.

Louis XIV of France, who had many bastard children and mistresses while married to his cousin, Queen Maria Theresa of Spain, settled down and married a common woman named Francoise when the Queen died. He stayed faithful to her until the day he died, despite his adulteress past.

Reference: (https://en.wikipedia.org/wiki/Fran%C3%A7oise_d%27Aubign%C3%A9,_Marquise_de_Maintenon)

993.

At various times before the modern period, India was producing more important scholarly works in Persian, such as dictionaries and commentaries, than Iran.

Reference: (https://baraza.cdrs.columbia.edu/indopersianhomelesstexts/)

994.

Bruce Willis released a Motown album in 1987.

Reference: (https://en.wikipedia.org/wiki/The_Return_of_Bruno_(album))

995.

You can pay the Jolly Roger Telephone Company to obnoxiously respond to robocalls. Subscribers can choose robot personalities, such as Whiskey Jack, who is frequently distracted by a game he is watching on television, or Salty Sally, a frazzled mother.

Reference: (https://www.nytimes.com/2017/05/11/smarter-living/stop-robocalls.html)

996.

There is a broom closet inside Cheyenne Mountain Complex called "Stargate Command".

Reference: (https://en.wikipedia.org/wiki/Cheyenne_Mountain_Complex#In_popular_culture)

997.

An island in the Caribbean named Montserrat not only celebrates St. Patrick's Day as a national holiday like Ireland, but also has a 2 week carnival leading up to it.

Reference: (http://www.thejournal.ie/readme/st-patricks-day-montserrat-2662360-Mar2016/)

998.

"Candle in the Wind" was not written for Princess Diana, but rather Marilyn Monroe in 1974. The song's opening line "Goodbye, Norma Jean" refers to Monroe's real name, Norma Jeane.

Reference: (https://en.wikipedia.org/wiki/Candle_in_the_Wind)

999.

The Sonic Hedgehog gene is vital for left and right brain development. Scientists have been trying to change the name for decades but it seems like it's here to stay.

Reference: (https://nerdist.com/sonic-the-hedgehog-has-a-gene-named-after-him-but-what-does-it-do/)

1000.

The Great Mosque of Djenne, considered by many to be one of the greatest landmarks in Africa, was built in 1906 by the French.

Reference: (https://en.wikipedia.org/wiki/Great_Mosque_of_Djenn%C3%A9)

Printed in Great Britain
by Amazon